JUDGE ADVOCATE ELLIS BENT
Letters and Diaries 1809-1811

JUDGE ADVOCATE ELLIS BENT
Letters and Diaries 1809-1811

Edited by
Paula Jane Byrne

Foreword by Bruce Kercher

DESERT PEA PRESS

2012

Published in Sydney by

Published in Sydney by
Desert Pea Press
an imprint of The Federation Press
PO Box 45, Annandale, NSW, 2038.
71 John St, Leichhardt, NSW, 2040.
Ph (02) 9552 2200. Fax (02) 9552 1681
E-mail: info@federationpress.com.au
Website: http://www.federationpress.com.au

National Library of Australia Cataloguing-in-Publication entry

Byrne, Paula Jane

Judge Advocate Ellis Bent : letters and diaries 1809-1811 / Paula Jane Byrne
Includes index.
ISBN 978 187686 110 0

Bent, Ellis, 1783-1815 – Correspondence.
Dromedary (Ship).
Judges – New South Wales – Correspondence.
Madeira Islands – Description and travel.
Praia (Cape Verde) – Description and travel.
Rio de Janeiro (Brazil) – Description and travel.

347.94014

Typeset by Limedesign, Turramurra, NSW.
Printed by Griffin Press, Adelaide, SA.

Foreword

When the young Ellis Bent sailed into Port Jackson at the end of 1809, he carried with him the traditions of English law and a determination to put it into effect. Two years earlier, the colony's only military coup had deposed Governor Bligh and with it the legal underpinnings of the colony's courts. Governor Macquarie was sent to restore formal British government, and Bent to restore the lawful operation of the colony's courts. Bent was the colony's new Judge Advocate, to preside over all the courts.

Ellis Bent was the first barrister to hold judicial office in New South Wales. He succeeded the gentleman amateur Richard Atkins who had been Judge Advocate off and on since 1796. Like Governor Bligh, Atkins was deposed by the military officers who illegally assumed government on the colony's 20th anniversary, 26 January 1808. After that a series of military officers acted as Judge Advocate for the rest of 1808. A year later, the rebels reappointed Atkins, having found that no one else had his skills. For most of 1809, Atkins continued judicial work as if nothing had changed.

Atkins had legal skills, but no qualifications in law. Only one of the Judge Advocates since 1788 had been legally qualified, Richard Dore, an attorney, who was on the colonial bench between 1798 and his death in 1800. The others, Collins and Atkins, were legal amateurs, who applied the complexities of English law to the unprecedented circumstances of a convict colony. Collins and Atkins had followed the general standards and many of the technical rules of English law, but had often altered the law to suit the conditions of the colony. The rules of reception of English law allowed some variation from the parent law, but only by omission of unsuitable laws. Collins and Atkins went further than that when they created new law for the colony. This was unlawful by English standards, but apparently tolerated by the British government. Nor was the Privy Council able to intervene: there was only one fully heard and decided appeal from New South Wales to that body in the colony's first 20 years (see *Lord, attorney for Mechan v. Palmer* [1803] NSWKR 3).

Variations in laws may have been tolerable, but what could not be tolerated was the complete overthrow of the colony's government, even if the rebels kept up the form of the courts. The coup brought the colony's curious legal status to a crisis, resulting in the appointment of Ellis Bent to make clear that English propriety was to prevail.

As the letters in this remarkable volume show, Bent was determined to restore English law. He spent the next six years struggling to do so, sometimes finding that it was impossible. In particular, what would he do about the decisions made by the unlawfully constituted courts during the rebel period. Should the civil cases be reheard? Should those who had been imprisoned or flogged be allowed to sue for false imprisonment or assault? Bent met these issues with pragmatism as well as principle. Like Collins and Atkins, and like the celebrated first Chief Justice of New South Wales, Sir Francis Forbes, Bent found that it was necessary to adjust the application of English law in a new land.

Dr Paula Byrne is very well qualified for the task of editing the correspondence of Ellis Bent. She is the author of the ground breaking book, *Criminal Law and Colonial Subject: New South Wales, 1810-1830* (1993). In it, she showed the interaction of English law and the social circumstances of Britain's penal colony. Ellis Bent was Judge Advocate from 1810 to 1815. In this volume, Dr Byrne has returned to those years, through the fascinating correspondence of Australia's first fully qualified judge. The Francis Forbes Society for Australian Legal History is proud to publish this important work.

Bruce Kercher
President
Francis Forbes Society for Australian Legal History

Contents

LIST OF ILLUSTRATIONS

Portrait of Ellis Bent, MA, artist unknown, c1800,
National Library of Australia, nla pic-an 2265459.
Reproduced by permission of National Library.

Officer's mess room on board a ship of war, c1820,
National Library of Australia, nla pic-an 2838485.
Reproduced by permission of National Library.

Speaking a vessel off the Cape of Good Hope, Augustus Earle, 1824,
National Library of Australia, nla pic-an 2838467.
Reproduced by permission of National Library.

Vue de la salle de spectacle sur la place Do Rocio, Rio de Janeiro, Paris, 1822,
National Library of Australia, nla pic-an 9031302.
Reproduced by permission of National Library.

New South Wales, view of Sydney from the east side of the cove, John Heaviside
Clark, June 1810, National Library of Australia, nla pic-an 6016118.
Reproduced by permission of National Library.

Portrait of Ellis Bent, MA, artist unknown, c1800

Acknowledgements

The manuscripts of the Ellis Bent Journal and Letters are reproduced here with the kind permission of the Australian National Library. I would like to thank Graeme Powell and Paul Hetherington, both formerly of the library for their encouragement and enthusiasm for Ellis Bent. The project originated in my research into law and manners in the early colony, much aided by a Harold White Fellowship granted by the library. I thank also Susan Hall of the library for her help with copyright. This book is also a project of the *Francis Forbes Society for the Study of Legal History* in its wish to make widely available the early law records of the Colony of New South Wales. I am most grateful to Christopher Holt of The Federation Press for his introduction of the manuscript to the Society and for his continuing support of the project. Geoff Lindsay SC has been most gracious and helpful in bringing the letters and journal to a new audience. In editing the Journal I acknowledge the association with Professor Bruce Kercher, the advice and assistance of The Honourable John P Bryson QC and Dr Michael White QC and the members of the Forbes Society. Gillian Armitage and Kathryn Fitzhenry of The Federation Press provided excellent editorial advice and I am grateful for their forbearance.

Introduction

Judge Advocate Ellis Bent's observations on Governor Lachlan Macquarie's *Port Regulations* arrived on the Governor's desk in December 1814. These *Port Regulations* were to control the entry and exit of persons and goods at Port Jackson and were crucial in a trading port which was a part of the colonial circuit as well as a penal colony. Ellis Bent disagreed with many of Macquarie's proposals. In terms of the formation of government in New South Wales the disagreement between the two men is one of the most evocative in early colonial history. Ellis Bent wrote:

> I have set down in writing as Concisely as I could Such observations as were Suggested to me by a careful perusal of the draft I received from Your Excellency which observations I believe to be in perfect conformity with the law of England ... In so doing I have been under the necessity of referring to a variety of Acts of Parliament, which I am happy to communicate to Your Excellency if you are not already provided with them.[1]

In the first paragraph of his commentary Judge Advocate Bent noted that the *Port Regulations* should conform to the Plantation Laws 'all Governors being bound by oath to enforce these laws and being subject to severe penalty by deviation ...'. Again and again Bent referred to the 'illegality' of some of Governor Macquarie's proposals.

The labour involved in Bent's deliberations is apparent in the 'observations' document. In it Bent considers the crucial questions surrounding the person of the convict as compared to a free British subject. It was a perspective that Governor Macquarie would have difficulty comprehending. Macquarie's own administrative experience derived from the military where orderly tent cities were set up and administered by military commanders.[2] The idea of regulation came easily to Macquarie and ordering 'regulations of convenience' was something he had done

from his first days in Sydney. Bakers, boat owners, public houses were all
to be licensed and these listings of persons are to be found in the Bonwick
transcripts. In a sense all military men were able to be visionaries and
Governors were enabled by their Commissions to put their ideas into
practice and regulation.[3] Such regulating was only to become difficult when
it confronted the law of England. Macquarie had no doubt as to whose
views would prevail. Some of Bent's suggestions he applied, others he
completely ignored. The regulations concerning the movement of persons
in and out of the colony were those that were most contrary to Bent's
understanding of the liberty of the person. However, it was more than
this difference of definition that mattered. Macquarie's personal complaint
against Ellis Bent resulting from this dispute draws us utterly into the world
of the 18th and early 19th century.

> Mr Bent and his family left England and arrived here in the same
> ship with me (His Majesty's Ship Dromedary) on the 28 December
> 1809; and the familiar and friendly intercourses which commenced
> between us and our respective Families were prolonged without
> Material interruption until 16 December 1813 ... during the whole
> course of which period, I continued to extend to him and his family
> every good Office, Civility and Attention within my power ...[4]

Macquarie detailed a disagreement over the construction of a Court
House, where funds from subscribers were insufficient to cover the cost.

> From this period he Ceased to visit me in his Usual familiar way; and
> when I had Occasion to send for him on public business he assumed
> a very marked Degree of Coolness and Reserve in his manner.[5]

Bent informed Macquarie that his manner was indeed because
a Court House had not been built. Macquarie had 'shewn a great Want
of feeling for his Situation and personal comfort as Judge Advocate'.[6]
According to Governor Macquarie after this exchange Ellis Bent refused to
stay in town when ordered, refused to stand when Macquarie entered the
church and did not ask permission to sell land that had been granted to him.
Of the observations on the Port Regulations Macquarie said he was 'hurt'.

In this dispute we find a landscape of emotion and custom, not easily read in the 21st century. Ellis Bent came to see himself and his position as a counterpoint to the authority of the Governor. The language he referred to – 'legal', 'free British Subjects', 'liberties and conveniences', 'comfort' – may be contrasted with Macquarie's 'honour and authority' and his notion of 'disrespect'. They are two different ways of seeing the colony and from Ellis Bent's journal and letters it seems that such a collision of perspectives was inevitable. In his perusal of the colonies visited on the voyage to New South Wales Bent applied a similar perspective concerning the rights of the subject and the nature of authority. Lord Strangeford was 'disliked', he was a 'complete courtier'; the Prince Regent at Rio was detested, his government was one of 'complete favouritism'. These are formative ideas about institutional integrity and morality. It is a language of critique that would confront every colonial Governor. 'Autocracy' versus 'the public mind' would both appear in differing usages until the 1850s, but it was not language divorced from an extremely elaborate system of personal interaction where it was easy to be stung and hurt. It derived from the same world as Jane Austen's 'being out in public', or exposing oneself 'in some public place'.[7] So while the newspaper press appeared in the colony there was also this reference in letters and journals to this public that watched and tittered.

In Ellis Bent's journal and letters we are provided with a close insight into the expression and etiquette of power among the elite in the colonies. They give us the small gestures and objects by which a colonial administrator could be assured of respect and recognition.

These journals and many of the letters were written in a cabin on board the *Dromedary*, a troop ship which sailed from England in a diamond shaped convoy in early 1809. One accompanying ship was bound for Madeira and the other for the Cape. The ships had to remain together at all costs, despite the heavily laden *Hindostan* dragging its way behind them. The seas, one immediately feels on reading this journal, are far from open and spacious. They are crowded with other ships which suddenly veer into view and must at a time of war with France be clearly and quickly identified and shaped up to. They might be a prize which could be excitely taken for booty, a slave ship or an English ship with letters and information. It is Bent's letters and journals that give us most clearly the bristling world of the early 19th century, a world in which New South Wales is part of a vivid colonial circuit with goods and information flowing through it, whole lives and opportunities provided by the trading ports. A fat Cornish girl can become a Governor's mistress, a maid may leave a ship to take up a position as a milliner at Rio, a servant girl can 'get notions' at the Cape, anything is possible. The convoy first lands at Madeira, secondly spends 24 hours at Porto Praya, thirdly proceeds to Rio and finally to the Cape of Good Hope before reaching Sydney in early 1810. The Judge Advocate dines, shops and dances his way through these ports, describing Portuguese, Dutch and English modes of behaving in the colonies. He only feels the absence of a single adventuring life at Rio where he would have liked to go exploring, the custom of young officers everywhere. Bent and Macquarie arrive in Sydney to replace what they term the 'revolutionary' government, and there is some concern as to how this will be done. Joseph Banks felt the actions of Macarthur and the other officers 'bears evident marks of the Revolutionary proceedings of the French'[8] and Jamison appears 'agitated' when informed in Rio of these concerns.

C.H. Currey in *The Brothers Bent*[9] provides an outline of the lives of Ellis Bent and his brother Jeffery Hart Bent and this gives us some indication of the family history of a young man, born in 1783, who, along with his father, was able to use his connections well enough to obtain the position of Deputy Judge Advocate to New South Wales. Bent himself explained what was important about his history in a letter to Lord Liverpool in October 1811:

> In the earlier and more fortunate part of my life I was a Fellow Commoner of St Peters College Cambridge that after the usual resi-dence and examination I was admitted to take the degree of Bach-elor of Arts, and since that time I have taken the degree of, and at this moment am a Master of Arts at that University. Upon leaving College, I commenced the Study of the Law, and was admitted as a Fellow of the Society of Lincoln's Inn, by which I was called to the Bar in 1805, so that now I am a Barrister of nearly seven years stand-ing. Until I had the honour of being appointed by Lord Castlereagh to the situation I now hold, I regularly practiced the profession of the law, went on Northern Circuit and was one of the Senior Barris-ters of the Cumberland Sessions. The testimonials, I was at that time

required to present at your Lordships Office will I feel confident be deemed perfectly satisfactory to your Lordship.

In Ireland, I am well known to Viscount Northland, the Bishop of Derry, Sir Harry Bruce and others. In England to different Members of my own profession, to the Judge Advocate General to Lord G.H. Clarendon and my being in my present situation has been occasioned by Family misfortunes of the most serious nature.[10]

The family estate Moulsey had to be sold because of Bent's father's involvement in electoral fraud in the Aylesbury elections of 1802, his unseating from the House on petition and the subsequent decline in his fortunes, [11] referred to in the letters and journals here as 'Aylesbury' or 'the business at Aylesbury'. Robert Bent, a merchant dealing mainly with the lucrative West Indies trade had joined the Whig Club in 1797 and in 1802 was sought by some of the electors at Aylesbury, Buckinghamshire, to be a third choice in the elections of that year.[12] Robert Bent's agents had given 200 voters drink at a local tavern and these actions were the subject of investigation by the House of Commons and the Lords. Bent was described as a 'stranger' and the amount he spent was both celebrated by the electors and derided by his opponents. As we can see from these letters there was some sympathy for his predicament, electoral 'treating' was so common it was extremely difficult to legislate against. The young Ellis Bent was forced to leave England in an attempt to regain some of the family's wealth. Jane Austen best explains these young men from wealthy backgrounds with a career in law who 'made a very good appearance in the first circles, and drove about town in very knowing gigs'.[13] It is clear from his writing that Bent has many fashionable attitudes concerning taste, etiquette and politics that he and his friends were at the forefront of Whig ideas in England. One deplores Wellington, dislikes favouritism, and has the 'public' and liberty in mind. He, however, has quite a clinical view of slavery, reporting what he sees without the same kind of emotion expressed by his fellow traveller, Elizabeth Macquarie.[14] There is also, because of lack of means, a careful eye to expenditure and a willingness to note down discrepancies in prices, opportunities for investment and channels of influence.

The life continues in Sydney, larger than Cape Town, a pretty town. However, dissatisfaction, hinted at in Cape Town, starts to appear when he realises his place is not at the top of the Governor's table, not at the Governor's side but somewhere half way down among other colonial officials who seek favour, something Bent does not like to do. All through the voyage he has noted favouritism and being a courtier as strong negatives. He finds this again in New South Wales. The Court House was conflated with personal comfort; a building was not simply a building. When one looks at the remains of Macquarie's 'sandstone city' one must imagine these buildings as they were felt in the early 19th century, they were very much a part of human beings, the comfort, the flesh, of various colonial administrators. The barracks were favoured before a court; a hospital was favoured before a court. This was because of the great favour the Governor gave surgeon D'Arcy Wentworth, a wealthy man he appointed as Police Magistrate and who had narrowly avoided being transported as a convict for the offence of Highway Robbery.[15]

That the system of law operating in the colony was unworkable was something on which both Governor Macquarie and Ellis Bent agreed and it resulted in a long letter to England approved by Macquarie and referred to in these pages. C.H. Currey's *The Brothers Bent* suggests that the later conflict between the two men derived from the political structure of the colony – the various Commissions, those instructions received by each Governor, allowed them to do as they wished. Ellis Bent as Judge Advocate was reminded by Bathurst that as Judge Advocate he was in no position to question his Governor. Yet Ellis Bent acted as if he was a Judge, and possessed some independence.[16] Macquarie's response to the comments on the *Port Regulations* does seem to indicate a greater concern with his own authority than with English law and he was perhaps more ignorant of law than Currey allows. Both Bent and Macquarie agreed that emancipists should be able to practise law in the colony, yet for Bent it was only because there was no-one else who could. Both positions would harden, particularly after the arrival of Jeffery Hart Bent as Judge of the Supreme Court in the colony, and Currey's book sets out the resultant power play. It is John Ritchie who describes most clearly the kind of relationship the Colonial Office had to New South Wales. Sudden surges of interest, followed by periods of inertia and apathy resulted in a 'rickety and rackety' administration.[17] As Bent was castigated for the disrespect shown to his Governor, so was Macquarie warned to be mindful of

English law,[18] the contradiction remained unacknowledged. Alex Castles writes that the reasoning was diplomatic rather than legal and the matter of the relationship between government orders and English law would only be addressed at the end of the Macquarie period.[19] Ellis Bent also has diplomacy in mind in the few cases he discusses judging in these pages. He writes that he wants to stem the flow of civil cases that might result from the interregnum. It appears he does this by restricting the kinds of evidence required in cases surrounding financial transactions, plaintiffs needing the witnessing of a clerk or someone who could prove delivery. He required that promissory notes also needed a witness.[20] He also finds against persons whose cases would open a stream of litigation deriving from the revolution and refers in his letters to the important case involving Hook and Bent's own reasoning in it.[21] Bruce Kercher describes Bent's adherence to law in *Unruly Child* as well as his adapting to some of the exigencies of the local economy in spite of the Governor's directives.[22] The conflict between Bent and Macquarie did not result from personalities which are virtually impossible for the 21st century mind to perceive, nor did it result from clearly opposing political positions, it was more likely to have derived from the early 19th century manner of managing power that these journals and letters give us access to.

The historian Eiko Ikegami deals with flexibility and weak ties in the formation of civil society in Japan. She writes of 'open circuits' in social relations and prefers the term 'civility' rather than 'civil society' because she maintains 'civility implies a grammar of sociability' that is more suitable to her discussion of the emergence of proper public behaviour.[23] In Macquarie's 'personal complaint' and in the whole of Ellis Bent's journals and letters we can see a 'grammar of sociability' in a world that is rapidly changing. He provides us with the 'choreography of interpersonal communication', the 'regulation of conversational interaction and self preservation'.[24] It is a nervous, edgy world where one could see enormous implications in the flounce of a dress, the placing of a chair, the acceptance of a glass of wine. However, what distinguishes Bent from persons such as Marsden, Macarthur, Macquarie and later Francis Forbes is the inattention he pays to the spoken word. Insult is conveyed in actions rather than words. A carefully sewn baby's dress is returned to the Bent household, nothing is said. It is clear that Bent is capable of being flattered, that he expresses discontent, but he appears to feel no need to write down conversations. We see his dinner parties as if the participants are acting in mime, no subject of conversation is ever written about. What this does is show a realm of symbolic behaviour, a semiotics of non-verbal communication in the colony of New South Wales. Mary Putland is deeply disturbing, not only because of her new style of dressing in the transparent material of highly fashionable London, but because of her way of sitting down, her way of walking and carrying herself. She would be, he thought, a terrible political influence. It was where the dishes were placed on the table at a dinner of Elizabeth Macquarie that said so much about disregard for the representative of law in the colony.

In this arena of non-verbal communication appearance meant a great deal. The military was one means to change one's status in England. In New South Wales, the son of a draper such as a Macarthur could assume the status of gentry; Governor Macquarie's father had been a carpenter. Boswell writes Johnson's explanation of this when asked why no-one is angry at military men obtaining great wealth 'we are not angry at a soldier's getting riches because we see that he possesses qualities which we have not' and Boswell noted that military men 'acquire excellent habits of having all conveniences about them'.[25] It is the military style of living Ellis Bent most engages with in the colony, he absorbs the consumption patterns and the emphasis on display that fuels the colonial economy. We can list what is important to serve at dinner and how it was to be served. We can list the most important rooms in a house, the kind of musical instrument one had to have. If we were to consider the society as strung together by objects that gave the outward appearance of wealth and a circuit of dining where proper behaviour was to be expressed in the placement of guests, the body language indulged in and the quality of food, we are close to the ideals of Ellis Bent. Without the above, business, including the business of the courts and of government was fraught with tension. This world in microcosm inhabited the *Dromedary*. Days were ordered, protocols were strictly followed, both on board and in the ports visited. There was a kind of balance in it.

The journals Ellis Bent wrote were part of a tradition of writing about travel to amuse.[26] Bent himself had been an avid reader of Collins whose death he reports in these pages. Bent's own journal was written to amuse his family and friends and as such employs notions of the comic in his descriptions of the colonies he visits. This is particularly so in his discussion of the Catholic religion and its adherents, to a lesser extent he also is critical of looks, having a strong definition of ugliness. He is careful to copy his journal and letters, fearing that parts may have been lost. He also entertained the idea that one day his journals might be published, not his letters which contained too many personal observations of his contemporaries. This was not a vain hope when one considered Collins. At each port we also find him shopping and washing; carefully weighing up costs because he will sell these goods in New South Wales. Would he buy a little green monkey? No, perhaps not. It was not unusual to see monkeys in Sydney, nor cockatoos in London, and Bent relates the considerable trade in seeds and birds between the ports and in Sydney itself.

The colonies gave the impression to many that anything was possible, that riches could be quickly made and the past banished. This was why one went. Land was obtained for its cash value at resale even though one might act as if one had a country estate on the Nepean. Some did better than others, but it needed an astute person to ride even the lowest rung of credit and debt in New South Wales, that involving the exchange of rations or clothing from the government store. Bent saw this as lack of morality but he was quick to join such an economy, selling a land grant, trying to live as cheaply as possible with government men, accepting a house from the emancipist Andrew Thompson, hiring an emancipist clerk, seeking the services of an emancipist doctor. Failed commercial transactions were to be the stuff of the civil court, the resultant violence and argument that of the criminal courts. The colony was military driven, for military men and women the purpose of any travel outside of England was to amass a fortune; 'booty' is a word that frequently appears in Macquarie's journals.[27] In New South Wales the employment of emancipist agents, speculation in trade and land, the establishment of industry were the means by which money and fortune were to be obtained. This was attempted to be controlled by the fey world of manners that Bent so clearly describes. We also are given considerable information on the accounts of a gentleman. A lucky escape from the financial devastation of Bent's first agent was followed by placing all his money in the prestigious house of Mr Coutts to which he had been kindly recommended.

Bent deplored the negative 'party' as did most writers in this period, the colonies were to be haunted by cabals and cliques and women were likely to be part of both. Mary Putland, Commodore Bligh's daughter, was thought by Bent to have such a destructive potential in the colony. This allowing of women into the political realm as actors is apparent in other colonial diaries. Women, particularly loud military women, were active discussants of new ideas. That women were 'part' of political life in this manner broadens our understanding of early 19th century 'publics'. When Commodore Bligh failed to invite the Bents to several parties he was allowed to understand how offensive this had indeed been to the Judge Advocate. Bligh protested that as he was bringing many cases before the Judge Advocate he did not want the New South Wales 'publick' to believe there was a close relationship between the two men. Nonsense, writes Bent, the Commodore was not capable of 'so refined a sentiment'. It was the 'publick', which was in this discussion, the realm of what was good and right and this would appear often in colonial political debate. There was indeed little more than 'party' which indulged the passions and excitement of both men and women but both referred repeatedly to this public and wanted to access its 'mind'.[28]

New South Wales required assertion of status, against the military, against the Governor, and this status was expressed in possessions and in delicacy of speech and the use of silence. The self-positioning of Ellis Bent is set out in vivid detail in these journals. We can establish what was important in a house. A good entrance hall, proportions clearly given, a drawing room with 12 chairs set against the wall, a dining table. Ellis Bent also liked a house to be 'clean'. This requirement is quite new in English history for cleanliness was related only to clothing, not yet to the body and not yet to the household. He talks about bodily cleanliness only once. This word and others he uses such as 'plain' locate him in the Quaker influenced custom of living that became popular in the late 18th century as discussed by John Styles, plainness of dress and household decoration were adopted as indications of character.[29] The house of the former Judge Advocate, the aristocratic Atkins is 'dirty', on the voyage the Portuguese elite were 'dirty', Governor Macquarie's house is not 'as clean' as Ellis Bent's. The historian Felicity Heal has described how the English house began to be seen as a reflection of the integrity of the head of the household. The earlier hospitality that was required to be shown to all who appeared at the door was gradually replaced by charity for the poor and the use of the house to display the head of the household's power position. However, such display was fraught with tension, adequate performance was never easy.[30]

Bent's household in Sydney is very much shaped by the nature of the economy. He sees convict servants as saving him money and gives considerable detail on exactly how much is saved. Though their behaviour is argumentative, they are tolerated because of their cheapness. The need to save was the cause of the Bent's dispensing with Elizabeth who they had brought from England as a servant. This was a cash-nexus household, very modern in the relationship between servant and master. In England servants were primarily kin to their employer, in the colony this was not possible. When a young native girl is employed in Elizabeth's place it is the saving that is noticed first in Bent's journal – Elizabeth had become too expensive with her extravagant taste in clothes.

Bent is keen to obtain musical instruments and gives a long description of how a piano is shipped to New South Wales. It is Eliza, his wife, who plays and sings, for company. She does so 'prettily'. Mrs Paterson tried to sell him a broken pianola at a high price. Of bathing, water, the kitchen, the servant's quarters we hear nothing. Bent gives us a map of the material life of the colony; his own aesthetic is one of precise detail, it is selective. His descriptions of the Cape, a smaller settlement than Sydney, gives such detail about the different manners and customs of the Dutch.

For Ellis Bent the household was central, not only his own but also the Governor's with which he was 'intimate' until their argument. His household also included the offices of the court, which were in three sides of a square at the back of his house. In order to speak to Ellis Bent people had to wait in the front garden. Such waiting was by both Indigenous people and whites from different parts of the County of Cumberland. He describes 'Bennelong'[31] who 'is not dead' as Collins had written but who is a frequent visitor, too much so, if encouraged he 'would be constantly present'. For Ellis Bent this was an incorporation of Aboriginal people into 'friendship' and this word had quite a specific meaning in the early 19th century. Bent had few friends in the colony and they are part of some of his most emotive, almost passionate, discussions. The implications of offering Bungaree wine rather than spirits invokes all of the symbolism of wine in the construction of the English gentleman. As explained by Julie McIntyre, the offering of wine was both a challenge and an expression of equality.[32] Bent is both recognised by and recognising of Aboriginal politics, though he seems unclear on its exact implications. When a trial results in a deputation of Aboriginal people from Parramatta and Sydney we can never know where he was placed in the worldview of the deputation to his garden, and Aileen Moreton Robinson's view that to entangle or blend Indigenous and white perspectives is impossible is relevant here.[33] All we can say is that Aboriginal people from different language groups came to the court, some travelling some distance for the purpose. The camp fires Ellis Bent saw all along the coast were the camp fires of a political system that both surrounded and was part of the town. The incorporation of Indigenous people into the notion of friendship extended also to Maori who visited the town. Personal pique describes their actions according to Bent. For the historian 'friendship' obscures and it is easy to write history as if personal relationships were paramount, but such a move muffles a political history. The word 'friend' had different meanings in the 19th century than it has today. It is not possible to map such notions, either our own or Bent's on to Bennelong for example. Friendship is not a reciprocal notion between us and the people of Bent's time let alone a transcultural concept.

Flowing to and from the house were slips of paper, letters, documents, messages and this was the base of all human communication among the whites. Alan Atkinson argues that writing transformed the use of power in the late 17th and early 18th century, especially as it was exercised from the centre of the empire.[34] The Blue books of the colony carefully list the pens, paper, ink, ribbon required by each office of government. The importance of records of all kinds was demonstrated by their quick removal before Macquarie arrived, and the references to locked offices and missing lists. Though Bent makes much of his own writing and the extensive labour it required, he also had the use of a clerk. This was firstly George, a nephew of Joseph Banks, showing the importance of connection for employment. But George could neither spell nor write properly and so an emancipist clerk was obtained; an excellent man who had worked at law and who had been transported for forgery. The employment of civil clerks was unique to New South Wales.[35] The role these men played in interpreting the law for the ever litigious public was crucial. Cases resulted in fees, this was the way clerks and even Ellis Bent earned their money. These clerks were part of an emerging professional sphere which would include all departments of government. The civil clerks were the first to be called upon by any person seeking any form of contact with government and they were extremely helpful if the petitioner was illiterate. Their very accessibility partly explains the reach of the criminal and civil law in the early colony. It was only after 1823 that cases began to be described as trivial or vexatious.

When Ellis Bent arrived in New South Wales he claimed that proper legal records would be kept for the first time. It is to Bent that we are to be grateful for the massive number of volumes concerning wills, transferral of property and favours of those leaving the colony. When Bent writes that there were no legal records kept before his time he was incorrect, but if we consider the dating of his claim it appears quite soon after he arrived in the colony, when all official records had been removed from government offices and many of them packed up by Johnston and taken to England.[36] Bent saw himself as far more efficient than Atkins, his predecessor, and this perspective until recently has been adopted by historians. Since the work of Kercher, Dermody, Simpson and Atkinson, Atkins has been recognised as an imaginative and pragmatic Judge.[37] The Bench book of the Judge Advocate's Bench records all manner of approaches to the law and this is a continuance of Atkins' approachable style. Bent writes that this volume was taken down to the Governor every evening for his perusal. Bent explained to Liverpool the kind of culture that existed in the courtroom:

> The parties themselves appear in person to prosecute or defend the actions in which they are concerned, they bring into court with them all the passions and enmities towards each other by the effect of which Justice is most obstructed, order subverted, solemnity and decorum set at defiance and an inconceivable degree of discredit upon the proceedings and authority of the Court.[38]

If one locates law in popular understandings then this law is as valid as any other. While Bent was highly critical of the system he alone presided over, it was a product of Indigenous, free, convict and ex-convict understandings of what law was, what its purpose was, and what kind of results one could expect from it.

Ellis Bent collects and sells wine during the voyage to New South Wales. He had to sell through an agent. These agents, middlemen and women were key to the colony's economic survival. They, along with the taste and experimentation of the military, drive the day-to-day life of the colony and it is these agents who are so often in court to make use of its possibilities. The courts follow their lead and the practice of law is shaped around them and their clash or coalescence with what is understood as English law. As the anthropologist Lawrence Rosen writes about the basis of criminal and civil cases:

> Fact finding is partly about seeking truth, partly about defusing conflict, partly about maintaining a workable sense of being in the world – and all about stitching together law and culture so that each informs and supports the other.[39]

In the period before the 1814 Second Charter of Justice in New South Wales the courts in New South Wales were remarkably open to even the smallest of claims. Bent's role as Judge Advocate and the lack of local lawyers meant he was required at times to give advice to both prosecution and defence. In effect, he had to be the colony's Attorney General and court registrar as well as its judge. Beneath the military appearance of the government and even the military title of the judge, an intense trading atmosphere developed in the colony, resulting in a strong sense of rights and justice.

Paula Jane Byrne,
Editor

Endnotes

1   Macquarie to Bathurst, 24 February 1815, Enclosure 3, *Historical Records of Australia* (HRA), series 1, Vol. VIII, p. 401.

2   J. Ritchie, *Lachlan Macquarie, A Biography*, Melbourne University Press, Melbourne, 1986, p. 54.

3   C.H. Currey, *The Brothers Bent*, Sydney University Press, Sydney, 1968, p. 37.

4   Macquarie to Bathurst, 24 February 1815, HRA, 1, VIII, p. 391.

5   Ibid.

6   Ibid, p. 393.

7   J. Austen, *Sense and Sensibility*, Penguin, Harmondsworth ,1969, p. 127, *Pride and Prejudice*, Penguin, 1972, p. 257.

8   G. Mackaness, *Sir Joseph Banks*, Sydney University Press, Sydney, 1936, p. 94.

9   C.H. Currey, op.cit.

10 Bent to Liverpool, 30 November 1811, HRA, 1, IV, p. 67.

11 *The Times*, London, 2 June 1804.

12 R.G. Thorne, *The House of Commons, 1790–1820*, History of Parliament Trust, Secker and Warburg, London, 1986.

13 J. Austen, *Sense and Sensibility*, Penguin, Harmondsworth ,1969, p. 127.

14 Ritchie, op.cit., p. 116.

15 Ibid, pp.124,128.

16 Currey, op.cit.

17 Ritchie, op.cit., p. 106. A.G.L. Shaw, *Convicts and the Colonies*, Faber, London, 1966 gives a detailed history of this administration.

18 Currey, op.cit., pp. 77-78.

19 A.C. Castles, *An Australian Legal History*, Law Book Co., Sydney, 1982, pp. 35-36.

20 *Sydney Gazette*, 24 March 1810.

21 See letter to Jeffery Hart Bent, 2 May 1810.

22 B. Kercher, *An Unruly Child, A History of Law in Australia*, Allen and Unwin, Sydney, 1995, pp. 54-58.

23 E. Ikegami, *Bonds of Civility, Aesthetic Networks and the Political Origins of Japanese Culture*, Cambridge University Press, New York, 2005, p. 19.

24 J.E.Katz, M. Aakhus, *Perpetual Contact*, Cambridge University Press, Cambridge, 2002, p. xxxi.

25 James Boswell, *The Journal of a Tour to the Hebrides with Samuel Johnson*, Macdonald, London, 1785, pp. 286, 282.

26 M. Pratt, *Imperial Eyes*, Routledge, London, 1992.

27 Ritchie, *op.cit.*, p. 30.

28 P. Byrne, 'The Public Good: Competing Visions of Freedom in Colonial New South Wales', *Labour History*, May 1990, pp. 76-83.

29 J. Styles, *The Dress of the People*, Yale University Press, London, 2007, pp. 209-210.

30 F. Heal, *Hospitality in Early Modern England*, Clarendon, Oxford, 1990, pp. 6-15.

31 Bennelong told Governor Phillip that he had several names. This suggests a clan terminology and perhaps this Bennelong has the same name, it is difficult to tell. Phillip to Grenville, March 1790, *HRA,* 1, I, p.161.

32   J. McIntyre, 'Bannelong sat down with Governor Phillip and drank his wine and coffee as usual, Aborigines and wine', *History Australia*, Vol 5, No 2, 2008.

33   A. Moreton Robinson, 'I still call Australia Home: Indigenous belonging and place in a white postcolonizing society' in S. Ahmed, C. Cantaneda, A.M. Furtier and M. Sheller eds., *Uprootings/Regroundings, Questions of Home and Migration*, Berg, Oxford, 2003.

34   A.Atkinson, *The Europeans in Australia, A History, Volume One*, Oxford, Melbourne, 1998, pp. 19-36.

35   A. McMartin, *Public Servants and Patronage*, Sydney University Press, Sydney, 1983.

36   Macquarie to Castlereagh, 30 April 1810, HRA, 1, VII, p. 246.

37   This debate has been set out by Alan Atkinson, 'Richard Atkins The Women's Judge', *Journal of Australian Colonial History*, Vol 1, No. 1, pp. 115-142.

38   Bent to Liverpool, 19 October 1811, HRA, 1, VII, p. 60.

39   L. Rosen, *Law As Culture*, Princeton University Press, Princeton, 2006, p. 105.

A note on editing the manuscript

The letters and journals of Ellis Bent are held by the Australian National Library in Canberra. It is difficult to reduce a manuscript at any time, let alone one that has so many uses as Ellis Bent's. He is a gift for the material historian and I was reluctant to leave any small description out. He was a keen sailor, unlike Lachlan Macquarie for whom 'nothing' frequently happened, and I feel the descriptions of latitude and longitude will be of great interest to maritime historians. These days also, all of us are interested in temperature. What I have left out is repetition of information, albeit from the slightly different perspectives with which he writes to his mother or brother. I have also left out his continued and constant expressions of love for his family, often filling a paragraph of a letter; historians of emotion will find some accounts which are often repeated in the original manuscript. He labours a great deal on the jewellery of Brazil and the rituals of the Catholic Church for which he has a marked disdain. These also can be found in the original. I have also left spelling that captures the period, such as 'romantick', 'expence', 'domestick' 'shew' etc and have sought only to standardise place names and names of persons, 'Molesey' is replaced with its modern spelling 'Moulsey' 'Sidney' with 'Sydney' for example. I have modernised references to time and to points of the compass, 'One P.M' for example becomes 1pm, although variations in descriptions of time have been kept. 'W.S.W' becomes 'west south west'. Also, '&', used throughout becomes 'and'. I have declined always using Bent's continual dashes, replacing them often with separate sentences, however I have not sought to change his syntax or his unusual descriptive language, for example, 'of a pitch with their dress', believing that this gives an insight into the mentality of the period. He uses commas in an unusual manner and his capitalisation is sometimes erratic, but they both give some sense of his mind and meaning.

A brief biography of Ellis Bent

Ellis Bent was born in 1783. He was the son of a Liverpool West Indian merchant who developed strong connections with the Whig Club and was referred to in the House as a 'most respectable merchant'. Ellis Bent was educated at Cambridge and moved then to Lincoln's Inn, one of the Four Courts distinguished by its connection to Chancery. No-one at Lincoln's Inn needed to stand for a toast to the King, a special honour granted by Charles II after he was entertained there in 1672.[1] Bent was called to the Bar in 1805 and moved to the Northern Assizes on circuit during the winter months where he gained a reputation for skill. Such reputation and the failing of his father's business concerns led him to accept the position of Deputy Judge Advocate to the colony of New South Wales, following what was termed the 'Revolution' of the New South Wales Corps in 1808. After he arrived in the colony with Governor Macquarie in 1810 he was described as Judge Advocate of New South Wales. He held this position until his death in 1815. He died of 'dropsy of the chest', pneumonia, and was buried on Garden Island to which he had held a lease. His biography and that of his brother Jeffery Hart Bent was written by C.H. Currey in 1968.

Endnote

1   T. Tindale Daniell, *The Lawyers*, Gray's Inn, London, 1971, p. 161.

1

Journal of a Voyage

Commenced Friday May 19th 1809

At 11am embarked in a Boat at Portsmouth Point to go to the *Dromedary* at Spithead. Wind at south east and moderate; found that the *Dromedary* had sailed that morning from St Helen's being too heavily laden to go through the Needles. At 1pm we embarked on board the *Dromedary*[1] with S.S. Capt. Pritchard. In about half an hour Lieut. Colonel Macquarie, Governor of NSW, and his Lady came on board. At 3pm, the Commodore Captain Pascoe, of the *Hindostan*, gave the Signal for sailing. We weighed anchor – but the wind being very baffling, and changing to the west, obliged us to cast anchor again. Our Convoy consisted of H.M.S. *Hindostan* store Ship,[2] Captain Pascoe, Commodore, and H.M.S. *Dromedary*, Pritchard Esq. Acting Commander, both carrying part of the 73rd Regiment to N.S.W and the latter carrying the Governor and Judge Advocate of that Colony: and two transports, one for Madeira, and the other carrying Troops to the Cape. The Commodore and his wife drank tea on board the *Dromedary*.

Saturday May 20th

The Commodore came on board and announced his intention of putting out to sea again – but the wind proving very strong and foul, [he was] obliged to abandon the idea. The *Dromedary* was very much crowded having on board 592 Souls. Complaints made to the Colonel that the crowded situation of the soldiers would be very dangerous to their health in a hot Climate. The wind was rising to the west south west towards the night.

Sunday May 21st

Wind high and foul, still west by south, weather very squally. The badness of the Weather rendered it impossible to perform divine Service which I had consented to do at the request of the Governor and Captain. Preparations were made for increasing the accommodations of the soldiers by allowing them room on the Gun Deck.[3] A Message from the Commodore to come over with the *Dromedary's* Establishment. The Captain, Governor etc go on board the *Hindostan*.

Monday May 22nd

At 11am the Commodore came on board and announced his intention of sailing as the Wind was moderate and likely to change. At 12 the anchor was weighed and we got under way with a moderate Breeze from the South. At 6pm, the wind changed to west and sunk gradually. At 8pm we were off Dunmore. This day Two Shore Boats came to us, and I took the opportunity of dispatching some letters to those whom to have parted from will be my constant regret, and to remember, my greatest pleasure. We were not yet sufficiently settled to adopt any regular system of employing our time ...

Tuesday May 23rd

At 8 o'clock am The Needles bore north east by east during the night. The ship had passed the point of Dunrose, and was bearing down the Channel; but we were very much impeded by the *Hindostan* proving a very heavy sailor to our great vexation. At an early hour of the morning we spoke[4] H.M.S. the Fredericksteen, Captain Serle from Lisbon; but she brought no news from Sir Arthur Wellesley.[5] [At] 9am the Commodore spoke us and informed us that the French under Marshal Soult had abandoned Oporto.[6] Wind north east a pretty Breeze. At Noon the Commodore gave orders by Signal for us to set all sail and make two strange Vessels hoist their colours and shew their number. All sail set, [we] fired a gun – the Strangers hoisted Swedish Colours. At one asked permission to board, which was refused by the Commodore. At 2pm spoke the *Daisy* Gun Brig, and rejoined the Commodore. At 5pm received orders to sail astern of the Convoy. At 8pm The Bill[7] of Portland bore north east six leagues. At 10.30 retired to Bed – a fine Breeze at east by north.

Wednesday May 24th

At 4.30am off Stout Point, bearing north east 4 leagues distance. At 7.30 off Plymouth Harbour, the Rams Head bearing north, distant 1/4 leagues. A Boat came from shore, but I was too unwell to write, and the time was too short. The Commodore bore right ahead, distance 1 mile. The Convoy in her Quarters and the *Dromedary* astern, so that we sailed some what in the shape of a diamond. The *Hindostan* still continued to sail very heavily and we were often obliged to slacken sail for her, though she had every sail set, and we were only under reefed Top Sails. In the morning we changed numbers with the *Amethyst* Frigate, Captain Seymour, and the Fort off Plymouth. Poor Eliza[8] so ill as not to be able to rise at breakfast, and myself far from well. A fine, fresh Breeze at [from the] east. At noon we fell in with and changed numbers with H.M.S. *Swallow*, Captain Millner, who wished us a good voyage. At 3pm off the Lizard Point, bearing north west distant 6 Leagues. At 5pm we lost sight of the Lizard and with that of England. I must own I felt considerable regret on leaving the place of my birth and where I had left so many who were dear to me as relations and friends, and to whom I hoped I was also dear But whatever unpleasant and painful sensations of this nature I felt, were very transitory, quickly giving way to sanguine hopes of returning in a few years wiser and better, mellowed, not decayed, to enjoy in my native country an independence honourably earned. I stayed on the Poop, till I could no longer distinguish any part or speck of Land. At three o'clock the Commodore gave the signal to chase a strange Frigate[9] – all Sails were instantly set, and our number hoisted. But the Frigate hoisted Spanish colours and shewing her number in return we were recalled. Eliza got better in the course of the day and was able to dine with us, at 9pm passed within hail of the Commodore. All day the wind was remarkably fresh and fair, and we should have made great way had our Commodore been able to sail.

Thursday May 25th

At 6.30am fell in with two men of War, to the south east of us. We showed our number which was answered, they proved to be H.M.S. *Hero* of 74 guns, Captain Newman, and H.M.S. *Denmark* of 74 guns from off Rochefort, cruising. Our Commodore went on board the *Hero* during which time we hove to. The Wind was fresh and there was a heavy swell in the sea; the Ladies were very ill, and could not rise to Breakfast. At 8.30 made sail we were now off the Mouth of the Bay of Biscay, or in parallel with Ushant, but much to the West of it, steering West by South. The wind was fresh to the Southward and East on a Rough sea. The Motion of the Ship was very violent and increased by not being able to hoist more sail than reefed Top sails, on account of the Commodore sailing so badly tho' he had every sail set. My little boy very well and an excellent Sailor. Hearing that we should probably touch at Rio, [I am] determined to stay[10] at the Portuguese language which would hardly have been worth while, if we had been destined to stay only 3 or 4 days at Madeira. At 11.15pm passed the Commodore within Hail who informed us that Sir A. Wellesly had defeated the French under Marshal Soult, with the loss of 20,000 Men that General Raget had lost an arm, that the English had lost possession of Oporto, and the French were in Gizon. That Joseph Buonaparte had left Madrid with the loss of 30,000 men; that Napoleon had been defeated by the Austrians, and that Admiral Cochrane had taken one line of Battle ship in the Saintes (West Indies) and a Frigate part of the L'Orient Squadron and the rest had escaped. At 11.45 made signal for the Convoy on our Starboard to keep her station – not obeying, touched her up with a gun. At noon we were in 68°.50 N. latitude and 8°.30' W. longlitude. The Lizard being north east 47 Leagues dis[tant] and Cape Finnisterre. south west 115 Leagues dis[tant], so that our average Sailing including all directions and delays during the last 24 hours was nearly as possible at the rate of 6 Miles an hour. At 3 pm Rain came on and the wind gradually fell till 8 o'clock when it became perfectly calm with a very heavy swell of the Sea. At ½ past 10 retired to Bed. Eliza had got better in the course of the day and was able to sit at dinner, but my Servants very ill particularly the Maid.

Friday May 26th

At 3am the wind freshened – at 4 Commodore ordered us to reconnoitre two strange sail – all sail set and made chace, informed them by Signal that they appeared to be a Man of War and a Frigate. Shewed our number to them and hoisted our private Signal, which they would not answer. At ½ past 7 Commodore recalled us by Signal. At 8 o'clock the ship being very suspicious and not hoisting their Signal the Commodore gave the Signal to prepare for battle. All hands up. Wind very high at south east with much rain, a thick haze coming in, at 9 lost sight of them. At 10 Wind and Rain increased at 11 veered to south by west and blew a heavy Gale accompanied with a great Swell. I offered my services to the Captain who appointed me to assist in the Cockpit, and I requested I might be employed on the Quarter Deck. At 12 the strange Sail again seen but a good deal leeward.

Monday May 29th

Shortly after 12 am on Friday last, the Gale increased so much and the Swell was so high as to render it impossible to stand or sit without taking fast hold of something. The vessel was Gunnel to and every wave broke over us. The Commodore's Main Top Sail was split – and our Fore Hay Sail was shivered to Rags. The Strange Sail still continued to chase us and caused us much trouble, altho' we were in the highest spirits. During the night the Wind increased and the Vessel rocked so violently that my Bed and myself were three times thrown from one side of the Cabin to the other. Everything was obliged to be lashed down. On Saturday the strange Sail disappeared whether they answered the Commodore's private Signal or not we do not know. The Wind became more moderate but was still foul and the heavy sea had coaxed us into the Bay of Biscay. On Sunday the Wind more moderate, but the Sea very heavy and motion very violent. A soldier was flogged by the Boatswain for insolence to his superior officer. This day at 4am the wind blew fair, but we were now 80 miles from Cape Finnisterre than on Thursday last. At 10am the Boatswain by Colonel Macquarie's orders flogged 7 soldiers for deserting their watch. At ½ past one, a strange Sail hove in sight 12 miles to leeward. At ¼ before 2 chased her by Signal from

Commodore at 2 gained fast on her at ¼ past two the Commodore hoisted French colours and we did the like. At three informed Commodore by signal that she was a suspicious Ship – fired a shot at her, in ten minutes fired another. At ¼ past 3 joined the wind and neared her, fired a shot under her stern. She shortened sail and hove to. At 4 went to dinner – at ¼ past 4 fired and prepared a Broad side. Five minutes after she struck[11]. She proved to be the *Gustavus* from St Bartholomew's an American Ship, fast sailor, Copper bottomed, trading under Swedish colours, taken by a French Privateer[12] 5 days before, loaded down with a valuable Cargo of Cotton and Rice 350 tons Berthen. We took possession of her and sailed after the Commodore whom we soon reached and made all sail on our course.

Tuesday May 30th

At 3am made sail after a strange ship, at 4 fired two guns, at 6 boarded her and she proved to be the *Harlequin* English Schooner from Guernsey. The Commodore resolved to send the *Gustavus* into Portsmouth. Sent the first Sheet of my Journal to my Mother in a letter and also wrote to my Brother by the Prize we took on the preceding day, and which was sent to Portsmouth by the *Harlequin*. A great part of this day was lost by the delay for sending off the Prize, and towards evening the Wind changed. Situation at noon Sat 45 53' N Long 9' 48 W Cape Finnisterre S 5 E 138 mile distant.

Thursday June 1st

At 5 o'clock am the wind changed suddenly in our favour, but still blew very strong indeed accompanied with a tremendous swell of the sea, which rendered it impossible to stand or sit. Unfortunately our ship was obliged to lie for the Commodore who was engaged in examining some American ships at one of which we fired two shot, brought her under astern and spoke her detained her until the Commodore did the same. He finding she was no prize allowed her to proceed. During the day, the wind moderated, and towards evening the wind had subsided considerably, though still very unpleasant situation at Noon at 45 7 N Long 10' 15 N Cape Finnisterre S 16 E Distance 142 miles.

Friday June 2nd

Very little Wind in the morning, but that fair. During the Day the Commodore paid us a visit and towards Evening it became calm with a heavy swell in the Sea at night a little Wind rose, but unfortunately contrary to us. We all began to be pretty well tired of the Bay of Biscay on which we had suffered so much bad weather. By the above account our progress will be seen to have been very slow our situation this day at Noon was as follows. Lat 43, 40' Long 11 41' W Cape Finnisterre bearing S 56 E distant 73 miles.

Saturday June 3rd

At 8am Wind very fresh and foul accompanied with much Rain under a heavy Sea. And all our hopes were much damped and we feared we should have to hear as we could the mortification of being driven further into the Bay of Biscay when on the point of doubling Cape Finnisterre. But at noon it cleared up, the Wind changing some points in our favour, and the Captain rejoiced us exceedingly by communicating to us that we had cleared the Bay and were to the south of Cape Finnisterre, for we were expecting another unpleasant Gale of Wind and sleepless night like that of Wednesday last. Our situation at Noon at which time all our nautical observations are made was as follows Lat 43°, 24 N. Long 12°, 13 W. Cape Finnisterre bearing South 73° East distant 111 miles so that we were almost to the Eastward of that Cape and now sailing down the Coast with a fine North West Wind.

Sunday June 4th

The wind unfortunately changed this morning and blew very violently. About 6pm it blew a hard Gale, nothing could exceed the confusion in which we were. Tables and chairs were breaking loose from their lashings – dishes, glasses, maps, thermometers flying about the room breaking into a thousand pieces. Poor Eliza missing her Hold was unfortunately thrown from one side of the cabin to the other, and had a narrow escape as her Head came close to the Bulk Head. However, she was lucky enough to receive only some slight bruises and suffer much fright. The Gale was very violent during the night, not a wink of sleep to be got. My little Boy however was not disturbed but slept like a Top all night. We were all glad when morning came.

Monday June 5th

At 8 o'clock we breakfasted, the Weather was still squally and the swell very high so that the motion of the Vessel was very great. But there was more inconvenience than Danger. The Wind was gradually dropping and the sea outriding. During the preceding day we had not made much progress and though the Wind was favourable the swell of the Sea being against us, much impeded us. At noon Cape Finnisterre was 28 leagues to the East of us. During the day we fired 6 shot at a strange Vessel, the last of which was coming close to her. She hove to in our stern and proved to be an American. The Commodore dismissed her, being satisfied with our[13] answers.

Tuesday June 6th

At 9am the Commodore ordered us to pass within Hail. At half past 9 he spoke us that at 10 o'clock of the preceding night one of our convoy had been attacked by a French Privateer which fired several Shot at her, but had at last steered off on approach of the *Hindostan*. I forgot to note that on Sunday we fell in with his M.S. *Magicienne*, Captain Croytes and her convoy of 10 sail for the East Indies. Our Commodore having on board the Boatswain of the *Magicienne* and letters for her Captain sent a Boat with them. But the sea was so high that the Boat was soon swamped and the Boatswain and two men with the dispatches lost. In consequence of the attack upon the *Oxford,* the Commodore ordered us to look out 6 miles on his Weather Bow during the day and to lead the Convoy with a light during the night. James McDonald, Tailor, died and was buried this day. The Captain reading service. The Wind during this day was moderate and the sea tolerably smooth, and we had a quiet night. At noon we were south of Oporto.

Wednesday June 7th

The Swell this day is entirely gone down and the Wind very moderate but fair, passed within Hail of our Commodore who ordered our Captain on Board, to be present at a Survey and condemnation of some sails and provisions. At Noon it was almost calm. The soldiers clothing in the Hold sustained considerable damage in the late bad weather. At 2 o'clock pm a soldier was flogged for drunkenness and received 24 severe lashes from the Boatswain. At Noon we were still to the north of Lisbon.

Thursday June 8th

A very fine Wind sprung up in the morning. The bad sailing of the Commodore's Ship prevented us from reaping the full benefit. It was ascertained that the quickest sailing the *Hindostan* could reach was 7 miles an Hour, and when the Wind enabled us to sail 7 knots an hour, the *Dromedary* would fetch 12 with half the canvas. At Nine brought to an American brig from Lisbon. The evening before it was bound to the Marble Head in America. She informed us that not a single Frenchman remained in Portugal. The Captain brought a Chest of very fine oranges for our Mess which contained about 400 very few of which were unsound. The price of the chest was 35 shillings. In the course of the day we brought to another American who told us there were 46 sail of American vessels at Madeira – that Provisions there were plentiful and cheap. At Noon we were 400 miles from Madeira which bore S 34 W which was the exact course the Wind enabled us to steer. In the evening the Wind was very fine and fresh and we sailed under two Topsails 7 knots an Hour without any aberrant motion of the vessel. The *Hindostan* had every sail set.

Friday June 9th

The Wind had been fair during the whole night and was so this morning but though we had only the fore and main top sails set, the *Hindostan* was greatly behind us. At 10am a Black Soldier of the Band punished with a dozen for stealing. At Noon we found that we had sailed during the last 24 hours 168 Miles, and that we were about 276 Miles from Madeira. We all dined at the Officer's mess, and passed a very comfortable day, Mrs Macquarie myself and Eliza were each fined a dozen of Wine, as it was the first time we had ever dined at Soldier's mess. At 5 o'clock brought to and spoke the *Oxford* Transport one of our Convoy bound to the Cape with Troops. Captain Wallis of the 21st Dragoons came on board with a Sailor of that vessel in Irons on the following account. This sailor having behaved very insolently to the Captain had been sent some days ago on board the *Hindostan* for punishment. But having bravely been the first to volunteer to go in a Boat and attempt to save the lives of the crew of the Boat belonging to the ship which was swamped on Sunday last the Commodore had pardoned him and sent him back to the Ship but this day he unprovokedly knocked down a Corporal and being ordered to be put in Irons he ran to the Gangway and threw himself into the Sea. Being picked up he was sent on board and was unmanageable. At Six we spoke the *Hindostan* and the Commodore refused to receive the Man that night and he was therefore kept in Irons and Captain Wallis was obliged to sleep on board the *Dromedary*. With respect to the Boat's Crew of the Hindostan part of which was lost on Sunday last I must record a remarkable instance of the courage and generosity of the British sailor. He was himself one of the Crew on duty on the boat when the sea broke into it and swamped it; and 9 Sailors were washed into the Sea. He was immediately picked up and restored to his Ship; but seeing Four of his Messmates struggling in vain to save themselves; crying out, Damned if the Mess shall be spoiled, he threw himself into a most tremendous Sea and fortunately succeeded in saving their lives, without losing his own. The Officers on board the *Hindostan* immediately made up for him a purse of twenty Guineas.

Saturday June 10th

At 8 o'clock am found the Log board that we had made 128 miles since the preceding Noon. During all this time, we were sailing under two double reefed Top Sails while the *Hindostan* had every sail set. At 8.30am Commodore ordered us by Signal to look out west by north for land. At

Noon, by observation, we were in lat 34 04' N Long 15 32' W. Porto Santo bearing distant 96 miles. We found that in the last 24 hours we had run to 156 miles. At 1 o'clock the Commodore ordered us to make all sail south west until 7 o'clock for land . And at that time to heave to. Made sail immediately At 7 o'clock we layed.

Sunday June 11th

Frequent Squalls of Rain took place during the night and morning. About 4 o'clock am we made sail and at 10.30am we made the Island of Porto Santo one of the Madeiras bearing north-north west 10 distant 30 miles. At 11.15am to our great joy we came in sight of the Island of Madeira bearing west distant 21 miles. We were at this time considerably ahead of the Commodore as a consequence of his repeating his Signal this morning to make Sail for Land. Therefore we shortened sail to enable him and the Convoy to come up with us. At 1.30 we found we had mistaken the Desertas high Rocks to the south of Madeira for that land and had consequently sailed greatly to Leeward. We were unable on account of the Squally Weather to reach that Island that night, to our great mortification, and therefore we lay to after having rounded the Desertas. At 3am Monday morning we made sail and at 5 o'clock we anchored safely in Funchal Road opposite that beautiful and romantic town.

Endnotes

1 The *Dromedary* was an English Man O' War. There were six classes of these ships and the *Dromedary* was a ship of the fourth class. It carried 40-60 guns. Fourth class ships were small two decked ships and were too lightly armed to stand in the line of battle so they were employed as escorts or used to undertake naval operations in shallow waters. These ships were about 146 feet long on the gun deck and 41 feet in breadth. Their average speed was between 8 and 9 knots. The *Dromedary* was formerly named the *Janus* before its conversion in 1788 into a 21 gun storeship. In 1800 it was deployed in the West Indies as a troopship. See P. Goodwin, *Men O' War*, Carlton Books, London, 2003. The *Dromedary* here is being used as a troop transport; it is therefore crowded and uncomfortable for the soldiers. Not for Bent, however. In the late 18th and early 19th centuries the new English colonies in India, the 'far east' and America led to an increase in sea travel. The wealthy paid for cabins which were built for them and which they furnished themselves. This furniture was often sold at the destination. This is one

of the reasons for the existence of good furniture in the colonies. Bent is not a paying passenger, but his accommodation on board follows that pattern. See G.P.B Naish and H. Amery, *The Age of Sailing Ships*, Usborne, Chicago, 1976 and K. Chatterton, *Sailing Ships*, Sidgewick and Jackson, London, 1909.

2   The storeship was much slower.

3   The health of sailors had been a concern from the late 18th century. See G. Dening, *Mr Bligh's Bad Language*, Cambridge University Press, Cambridge, 1992.

4   'Spoke' means to call from one ship to another.

5   This is the famous Wellington, Arthur Wellesley, First Duke of Wellington. His commission had begun in 1789 but he achieved his first distinction in India where he held independent command in the Maharatta Wars. If you read the *Sydney Gazette* from this period you will realise how avidly the exploits of these military commanders were followed. They were the celebrities of the 18th and early 19th centuries. However, unlike today's military they were also severely criticised by the popular press for their decisions, their comedies and their heroic acts. Wellesley was often before military courts for his decisions.

6   Wellesley 'had taken over the command of the English army at Coimbra in the north of Portugal, he had 37,000 men. He left 12,000 to guard the Tagus and directed 8,000 under Beresford on Lamengo, to pass the Duero and descend on the right bank, he moved with the remainder on Oporto. The advance began on the 6 May. Soult, French commander was hemmed in by insurgent bands, he had been forced to scatter his troops and had only 10,000 men with him in Oporto. He knew nothing of the danger threatening him until the 10th when a French division on the Vouga was attacked and driven in. He then destroyed the bridge over the Duero, seized all the boats near Oporto, and made arrangements for retreat. On the 12th Wellesley forced the passage of the river. Three boats were obtained by Colonel John Waters and three companies took the Seminary, a large building on the right bank. More troops followed them, while others passed the river three miles higher up. After trying in vain to recover the Seminary, the French retired in disorder from the city. Soult found that his intended line of retreat was barred by Beresford; so he destroyed his guns, abandoned his stores, took a path over the mountains and on the 19th crossed the frontier into Galacia'. See the *Dictionary of National Biography*, Macmillan, London, 1885, Vol. XX, p.1086.

7   Narrow promontory.

8   His wife Eliza Bent nee Bunster, a Master Mariner's daughter.

9   A frigate is a small ship relying on oars as well as sails, in the 17th century the frigate proper as a fast cruiser was introduced by the British navy. See Chatterton, *op.cit*, pp. 205, 252.

10   Continue learning.

11   Surrendered.

12   Privateers were privately owned ships that behaved in a manner similar to pirates. They, however, had the permission of the navy to prey upon merchant shipping of enemy countries. See R. O'Neill, *Patrick O'Brien's Navy*, Salamander Books, Baltimore, 2003.

13   That is 'the answers we received'.

2

Letters from the Voyage to Madeira

To Mother, May 9 1809

We have a Cabin to ourselves and the use of another but they do not equal my expectations tho' they are very tolerable. I have in mine what I was obliged to buy, a good Sofa, Chest of Drawers and Wash hand Stand. In consequence of the vessel having dropt down to these Roads, Eliza, my little boy, her maid and myself came here 12 miles in an open Boat, Eliza was a good deal frightened…

To Mother May 22 1809

We rise early in order to breakfast at 8 o'clock. Our party is small, consisting of Colonel Macquarie, his wife, the Captain, a young midshipman of the name of Goodall, Eliza and myself. We have Coffee, Tea, hot Rolls, Eggs, and cold meat. Whilst we are at Breakfast the Servants unswing our Cot, and remove it to the Poop, to air it. When Breakfast is over, the Room is then swept out. After Breakfast we amuse ourselves with reading, writing or walking on the Quarter Deck – At one we take some Bread and Cheese for Luncheon with a Glass of Porter – at 4 we dine – our dinner is good and well cooked. Yesterday we had Soup, Boiled Beef, roast Ducks, curry and asparagus, broccoli and plum pudding – Port and sherry and a desert of raisins. We do not drink much or have Coffee, shortly after dinner and Tea after that. At nine we have some Supper, at ten or 1/2 past we retire to Bed. Eliza and the little Boy sleep in the Cot and I am in a very nice couch bed belonging to the Captain. Till now we have been very busy in arranging our room and disposing our clothes in the Drawers. Elizabeth and Mrs Macquarie's maid have a Cabin to themselves, but with the ship so crowded that George has hitherto been obliged to sleep on a Box on the Deck, tonight he will get a Berth. We have on board 592 Souls, A Quantity of sheep, chickens and Fowls in abundance. When we get out to Sea, no light is allowed in the ship after 10 o'clock by his Majesty's orders. I have this day commenced my Journal.

To Mother, May 30th 1809 Bay of Biscay

I am happy in having the opportunity of enclosing to you my Journal to the present moment and sending it by the Prize…Neither Eliza nor myself have been at all alarmed at meeting strange ships and preparing for battle as the last ship drew nearer our spirits encreased. She wished indeed to prevail upon me, not to go upon the Quarter Deck – but that was impossible – all cause of apprehension however soon terminated. When you have read my Journal I will thank you to let my friends Storks and Eliot etc see it. They will take care of it and return it to you.

To Jeffery Bent May 30th 1809

I have much pleasure in having an early opportunity of sending you news of us. We yesterday spied and gave chase to a Ship about 12 miles to windward of us. In about two hours we came up with her and fired away at her, mainly with nine Pounders. It was a fine sight …Five Days ago she was taken by a French Privateer and a French Prize Master was on board of her. The name of the Prize was Gustavus, Cargo and ship valued at £50,000, myself, Eliza, child and servants are all entitled to share. You will look after it and I request you to accept the proceeds which may involve £10 and upwards …. you have no idea what an animated scene preparations for Battle is – I did not feel the smallest alarms. The Prize is conveyed into Port by the Iris frigate, who is at this moment engaged in pursuing and firing at some ship or other.

3

Sketch of the Island of Madeira

In the hopes of contributing somewhat to your Amusement, I am venturing to give you such Ideas of the Island of Madeira, its Inhabitants, their Manners, and Customs, as struck my Mind, during the very short but agreeable stay there. I am aware that my own knowledge on this Subject must be very limited, that my description must be imperfect, and that my accuracy must be impeachable; but possibly you will read it with interest because I wrote it; and derive some entertainment from it, because it has afforded me amusement and has greatly relieved the monotony of this Scene.

This island then is situated in the Atlantic Ocean, in Latitude 32 37' 20" N and Longitude 16 55' 36" W. It has always been considered as forming part of Africa and has long been subject to the Kingdom of Portugal, by which country it was first discovered and colonized, about the year 1519. It is about 180 miles in circumference and it is composed of one immense Hill which may be seen at 14 or 15 Leagues distance. The whole Country is remarkably rugged, but much cultivated. The town of Funchal which (I believe) is the only one of the Island, is situated on the Southern part of it, on the Beach at the foot of the Mountain by which it is surrounded on all Sides. The situation is remarkably beautiful when seen from the Sea. Imagine to yourself a Town about the size of Guildford, consisting entirely of white Houses of various heights and appearances and stretching round a Little Bay of the Sea, each end of which is guarded by a Battery. Imagine, a very fine, broken, well wooded Mountain, covered with Vines and different Plants and Interspersed with Churches, Convents, Priories and the Country Houses of the Merchants, all white, and then fancy the perpetual ringing of Bells, and processions of priests and you will have a tolerable idea of Funchal. On entering however, the Pleasure that is felt by a distant Survey, is much diminished, for the Streets are uniformly narrow, not one exceeding Pater Naster Row in Width and the houses very mean and dirty in their appearance. Indeed after walking of half an hour along Lanes of the above description I could not help saying 'When shall we come to the town'. Thinking that I was not yet in the Suburbs. All the streets are paved with very rough, sharp stones, which renders it extremely painful for a stranger to walk and when I reached the Consul's house, my Feet were as sore and myself as fatigued, as if I had been walking a considerable distance for a wager. The Consul's House is in one of the Mean looking Streets I have been describing and has no external appearance whatever of respectability. Indeed there is one circumstance which considerably detracts from the appearance as well as cleanliness of all the Houses in Funchal. Instead of entering a comfortable Lobby or handsome Hall, with parlours on each side, as in England; all the Ground Floors are devoted to Offices or Store rooms, through which you have to walk, and ascend a dirty Staircase, with no carpet on it, before you can reach the Rooms where the Family live. This prevails in every house from highest to the lowest; but varying in point of cleanliness according to the character and circumstances of the Inhabitants. The nicest I had opportunity of observing was that occupied by the Commander in Chief, General Meade. The Entrance was adorned and kept cool by a number of tropical plants, such as bananas and plantains, and the Rooms, were lofty, cool, clean and well furnished. The Consul's House was also well furnished and some of the Rooms were very good particularly the Drawing Room which was a very well proportioned, lofty, Room. But this House was laid out in a clumsy straggling manner and was not kept very clean. The bedrooms abounding in Bugs and Fleas, with both of which Funchal is very well peopled. Excepting the Governor's house, which was a remarkably good one, the House belonging to Mr Page was the best looking in terms of external appearance, of any I saw, and it seemed to be cleaner on the Inside. The only part of the Portuguese Governor's house that I saw was the Room appropriated for the attendance of Company before they were admitted. This was a remarkably fine Hall, very spacious and cool and commanding a beautiful sea view. The Great Object in Madeira as in all hot climates is to keep the Houses cool, in which they succeed very well. In the first place the Streets are so narrow, that one Row of houses is shaded from the Sun by the opposite Row, then the Houses themselves are remarkably thick. In the Summer time every Door and Window are thrown open, and the latter are protected by strong Venetian Blinds, which admit a current of air through every Room and obstruct the rays of the Sun. On this account

I found the houses much more comfortable, than an English House in the Summer time in which such precaution is taken.

In Funchal, where almost all the respectable people are English, the mode of living is also English.

In Mr V–'s house, the Meals were the same and conducted in the same style precisely. The Hour of dining is however, very late indeed. I think we never sat down to dinner before 7 o'clock or at the soonest half past 6 – But this custom, I am told has been introduced entirely by General Meade, (who keeps remarkably late hours, seldom rising before 12 o'clock or later) and that before his time the usual Dinner hour was three and never later than four. I must not omit mentioning one part of Madeira which is the most worthy of notice. This is the Parade, which is a very neat handsome kind of square. One side is occupied by a very good hospital; the opposite by different Houses very regular and neat, and the two Ends by the Cathedral Church of St Anthonio, the patron of the Island, and a Priory of Capuchin Monks. The Middle encloses a very excellent walk, each Side of which is adorned with different Trees, plants and Flowers peculiar to a warm Climate. The church of St Anthonio exhibits no external beauty, but is very handsome in the inside and profusely decorated with Gilding and Pictures and Images of Saints before whom a Lamp is constantly burning. The Pictures are by no means valuable or Specimens of Art. But what will most surprize a Person used to the crowded Streets of London and to the Sight of a long line of carriages, carts, wagons, etc. is the not seeing of any of these in Funchal, where the narrowness and steepness of the Streets totally preclude the use of such Vehicles. If these conveyances are not used in the Town, they are more particularly useless in the country where the almost perpendicular declivity of the Roads renders them in the highest degree, dangerous. Indeed it would be totally impossible for any quantity of horses or Mules to draw them. Throughout the island the Ladies are carried about in a hammock suspended from a long pole, in which they can either sit or lie down, or else in palaquins suspended in a similar manner in which they can only sit up. On the Pole there are usually Curtains to exclude the Sun. The gentlemen ride either upon Horses from America, or bred on the island, or on Mules, the two latter of which are remarkably safe. The hire of a Mule is usually Six Dollars a day, that of a Palanquin or Hammock which is always carried by two Men is very dear, depending entirely upon the distance. Luggage and heavy weights of every description are carried about on Trucks drawn by two Oxen, which are in general remarkably fine and docile, being guided with the utmost ease and dexterity by their Portuguese Drivers.

The shops in Funchal also present a very different appearance from those in England. Nothing of gay goods displayed with art, no parade or variety. The Shops here are Stores put together with no little confusion, and it requires some attention before a Person can discover a Shop from a mere private House. To this however there are some few exceptions. In Funchal there are few manufactures if any. They import all kinds of shoes and slops[1] of different kinds from England. The natives themselves seldom wear any shoes, which is a luxury confined to the higher orders.

There is in the town a Priory of Capuchins and a small convent, they are both poor, living chiefly on the alms of Individuals. Not far from the town, there is also a convent dedicated to St Clare, in a very beautiful Situation. Funchal abounds with Priests, who always appear in the dress of their order, namely a Black Gown and square Cap, and are ever treated with the profoundest respect by the Common People. They are very decent in their dress, and civil in their manners; but if I was informed aright, are not remarkable for their learning. I can only speak from hearsay of the Inns, which are two. But from some officers who were staying at them I learned that they were very dirty, badly furnished, affording no comforts of any kind and extremely dear. The Island of Madeira is a Bishopwick whose see is at Funchal. The Present Bishop is a native of the Brazils, and enjoys an income in right of his see, of about £2000 a year. He seldom lives at his house in Funchal, on account of his health and bears a very good character. At the head of the Civil Government of Madeira, is the Portuguese Governor who resides at the Government House at Funchal and presides over everything relating to Commerce and Revenue but does not meddle with the administration of Justice. This Department is remarkably deficient but I must from every account, do the Natives the Justice to say that there never was a set of people, who stood less in want of a criminal court. Overall civil processes, a Corregidor[2] or a Major presides and under him an inferior Judge, from whom there is an appeal to the Corregidor and from him to the King's Court which is now in Brazil. They each of them sit twice a week in Publick – but this is very uninteresting as every Suit is prosecuted in writing. There are no Courts in Madeira which take cognizance of the higher class of offences. And if Murder would be committed, the Murderer, and the prosecutor and their witnesses, must go to the Brazils, where alone the matter can be enquired into. Consequently all offenders of this description escape unpunished. Luckily indeed there are but few. Before the Emigration of the Court of Portugal to the Brazils, criminal justice was administered for the inhabitants of Madeira in Lisbon. Of the Police of Funchal I know nothing.

There appears to be a very good Custom House, where all goods exported or imported pay a certain ad valorum duty. This duty is paid annually by the different Wine Merchants as an accommodation both to themselves and the Officers.

Altho' we landed several trunks etc we were not at all troubled upon saying we belonged to an English Man of War. From this concise account of Funchal, it will be easily conceived that the town presents nothing very interesting either in the streets, the publick or private Buildings or the Shops. The Eye is very soon tired, of the dirt and exterior meanness of this Town. But of the Surrounding Country it is impossible to speak in terms too high. It is beautiful, romantick, and picturesque beyond description, nothing can exceed the boldness of the Scenery, the immense hills, the high Rocks, the deep ravines, the fine green of the Vines and other Trees, at once astonish and delight. The character of the Scenery is certainly grandeur, but a number of little shaded, cool, Glens abounding with wild strawberries, myrtles, geraniums and other beautiful plants add much softness to it. The season of our arrival was a dry one, so that the Beds of the mountain streams were empty but in Winter they are filled with torrents, which flowing from a great Elevation, descend with astonishing force, and often carry everything before them. The beds of these streams are remarkably deep, and I should have been tempted to doubt of their ever being filled, had I not seen the Ruins of a handsome Church and the remains of several houses, which had been swept away with their inhabitants only the last Season.

During my stay I had an opportunity of seeing a very beautiful place about two Miles from the town, called the Mount, the Country house of Mr Page one of the principal Wine Merchants in Funchal, and although I have often visited the Lakes, and seen some of the finest Welsh Scenery, I was never so struck by the Majesty and beauty of Nature. It is still situated about two Miles from the Town, the whole road being remarkably steep and rugged descent, affording every moment a fresh and apparently more beautiful view of the Roads of Funchal, the rocks of the Desertas, the Sea beyond and a very grand view of the Town and citadel and the surrounding country. I was very glad that I had not attempted to walk there for, exclusive of the distance, and the steepness of the Ascent, the Road itself was so rough, from being paved with very sharp stones, that I should certainly have disabled my shoes, and my Feet too, perhaps. I was therefore mounted upon a small and pretty gray pony who carried me up the Mountain at a footpace remarkably well. I thought the Road so steep, that on getting out of the Town, I was for dismounting to save the horse, but I was soon satisfied, that if that was my Plans, I might make up my Mind to walk all the way; and indeed, I afterward saw that it was the best part of the Road. E. who accompanied me was carried by two Portuguese in a Palanquin, and found it very commodious and pleasant mode of conveyance. The Bearers surprized me by their strength and activity, actually obliging me to stop them, that my Pony and I might not be left behind. The Road was bordered with Aloes, orange and Lemon Trees, plantains, bananas, and many shrubs and plants which were perfectly new to me, every now and then interrupted by a break affording a most delightful prospect. Mr Page's House was situated in a plantation of very fine Trees most of them Natives of a Tropical Climate. The house itself did not appear to be long, but very comfortable and well furnished. In Front a kind of portico at the outside of the Entrance Door, shaded by beautiful plants; there was a distinct view of the Harbour and every ship in it, and of the whole Town of Funchal. In the Portico there was a telescope fixed through which every object and especially Mr Page's Town House could be discerned with the utmost exactness. He has here also a Telegraph and another at the Town House by which he can maintain the easiest and quickest communication. He has about 40 acres of Garden Ground laid out in Gardens and plantations and grows everything that either Luxury or necessity can demand.

The Gardens and the mode of watering them were to me new and curious. They are upon a very steep acclivity and the Beds are below one another something like hanging Gardens. At the upper end there is what they call a Tank or reservoir of water; which being opened by a kind of Floodgate sends out a stream of water, which is conveyed by channels to the different Beds and equally distributed by the Gardeners to every part of them. This is absolutely necessary on account of the uncertain supply of rain which makes water here so valuable that the streams are let out at so much by the Hour by the person who takes the trouble to form the channel from the Mountains. Mr Page had every tree or plant that would come to perfection in the Soil, which was either ornamental or useful. Hedges of Myrtle of Geranium, of flowering shrubs and groves of oranges and lemons afforded shelter to numberless canary Birds, whose notes were much sweeter than the Song of those confined in Cages, and the groves were of the most delightful Fragrance. Indeed it was the most beautiful spot I ever saw. From thence we made a short excursion to the Mountain Church (higher up the Mountain) which is the first church in Funchal and is dedicated to St Anthonio. Its elevated situation commands a most extensive, varied and beautiful Prospect, comprehending the whole of that side of the Mountain, covered with Gentlemen's Seats, the town of Funchal, the harbour and shipping, and at greater distance the rocks of the Desertas, and the island of Porto Santo. The Rector (a Portuguese) and his wife, shewed us the Interior of this church, which like all Roman Catholic places of worship is profusely adorned with Gilding and Pictures. But the most remarkable object here is the Image of the Virgin Mary over the altar, to which an immense number of Pilgrims visit to pay their devotion and which is supposed to work all the miracles, that are, or that are supposed to be wrought in Madeira. This image consists neither more nor less than of a Doll, which is bought in London, covered with the most superb dress of satin. ... Such is the base superstition of the people, that they kneel and offer their all, almost to kiss the dress of this doll, made in London by their own order and at their own expense.

I had not an opportunity of making long excursions into the Country, which I am told, affords much in point of scenery worth attention, particularly a very beautiful Glen, called the Corral, which I regretted I could not visit. I must therefore finish here my account of the Country, but not without again expressing my delight, admiration, and astonishment at the romantick and sublime scenes which it presented to my view.

I will now proceed to give you some account of the production of this Island, with their miscellaneous circumstances that may introduce themselves.

The Principal Produce of Madeira, and the source of the wealth of the English Residents there is the Vine, the cultivation of which produces the most excellent Wine, and gives ease and opulence to a number of English Wine Merchants here. The Principal and most fruitful Vineyards are those on the Northern Part of the Island. They belong, however, not to the Wine Merchants themselves but to the Natives, who are themselves so poor, as not to be able to cultivate them, without the assistance of the Wine Merchants. These latter, therefore, supply the Owners of the Vineyards, with whom they are connected, (and who in consequence are obliged to send them all their Wine at stated price) with Vats, Presses, and occasionally with money. [Account of pressing process] this juice is then drawn off and put into Barrels and is what is called the Circeal [Sercial] or finest kind of Madeira being the result of the first squeezing of the Fruit. This Wine is not usually drunk much and is not that which is sent abroad. It is deemed a great Luxury and is handed about in small glasses during Dinner time, seldom making its appearance after but at the Tables of the extravagant. The fruit so squeezed is then put into a press and squeezed by Machinery which exhausts all the moisture of the Grape. This is also put into Barrels without any mixture whatever and sent on mules to Funchal. When this juice is obtained from picked Grapes, unmixed with any rotten ones, it is the prime Madeira. The wine is allowed to ferment before it is sent off to the Town. In the country it undergoes no adulteration, but when it arrives in Funchal, the Wine Merchants mix the best and the middling together and the whole with Brandy according to the different markets to which it is sent. This wine is not pressed from an eating Grape, it being rather too acid in that form. The Malmsey Madeira is pressed from a sweet Grape, entirely distinct from the other grape and is always pressed from the picked fruit. The Cerceal and Malmsey sell here from £70 to £80 per pipe. The Prime Madeira from £47 to £53 the Pipe.

Very little Corn of any kind is grown here, and there is but little pasturage; so that the island cannot provide for its Inhabitants with provisions. They obtain flour from America and during the embargo in that country were a good deal at a Loss, but at the time we were there in consequence of more than 50 Americans having been there, they had a great supply. All kinds of meat here is very scarce, and of course very dear, though very bad. The Beef is fed on oil cake and sells from 15d to

1/6 pr lb. Mutton is at the same price and equally poor. A great quantity of salted provisions is imported from England, Ireland and America. On this account you do not often meet with plain joints the Beef and Mutton generally coming on the Table in Stews, in which they excel. Poultry is also very dear here and sometimes not to be procured at all. You must now be thinking that the Inhabitants are badly off. But I must remind you that all the poor are Roman Catholicks and subsist in a great measure on Fish such as Mullet, herring and Mackarel of which they have plenty. Madeira also produces great plenty of all kinds of Vegetables and fruits except apples and pears; Peaches, Nectarines, the most beautiful mulberries, Apricots and bananas, figs, pomegranates and above all Grapes are in the greatest plenty.

With the Natives of the interior part of the Country, I had no opportunity of having Intercourse and in what I say of the Inhabitants, I mean therefore, those in the Town. The Men, then, appear to me to be remarkably well made, and strong limbed, their arms and legs being very muscular. Their faces are very dark, but of the European cast; their Eyes, black, their Hair, the same, and their noses, by no means flat. But they are far from handsome. Their Dress consists of a short cloth jacket and linen Trousers, usually tucked over their knees, and no shoes. Their Hats are large. In their ears, they wear gold rings. The Women are not so handsome as the Men, I think. Their Hat is a large cone like a Sugar Loaf with Broad Brims and they usually have ribbands of different colours about their Heads. The Remaining part of their Dress I cannot describe – but they are very fond of the Tawdry. I am now speaking of the common people only; of the highest class, I saw none except the men who conform to English Costume. They appeared to me very civil and obliging but I am told they are apt to be pert to their Masters, and will not bear to be spoken to too harshly ...

In my account of provisions I forgot to mention two principal articles, Bread and Butter; the first is very bad usually sour having no yeast. The butter is all salt from Ireland; even in the Consul's house we had not a morsel of fresh. Mr Page is almost the only person on the Island who has any and that is considered as a great rarity.

Endnotes

1   Slops are cheap clothing such as sailors and servants wore.
2   An administrative local position.

4

Letters from Madeira

To Mother June 15 1809

Funchall …
As soon as we cast anchor our Commodore saluted us with 15 guns which Salute was instantly returned by the same number.

We were soon surrounded by different shore Boats which brought us fresh Eggs, Bread, Butter, Strawberries, Cherries, Pomegranates, Lemons, oranges, Peaches, Nectarines, bananas and several other Tropical Fruits and the finest Vegetables – our Breakfast was very grateful indeed, as our Baker's bread is most terribly heavy, and our Hens have forgotten to lay Eggs. Leaving the Ladies on the ship Colonel Macquarie and myself were rowed to the shore in the Commodore's Cutter there being a continual surf on the Beach, we thought it better to try an easier Landing Place, altho' at a considerable distance from the Town and sailing around a most remarkable Rock, singular for its excessive Declivity and total Separation from the land we came on shore at an artificial landing Place at the bottom of another Rock to the Top of which we ascended by about a Hundred steps hewn out of it and walked along a steep road, in burning Sun and on the sharpest Pavement I ever felt.

… We first of all called upon the English Consul, who invited Colonel Macquarie and myself, with the Ladies to reside at his house, during our stay which of course we accepted. He is a young Man, pleasant, well informed, and unaffected. His name which I had almost forgotten to mention is Veitch and he lately married Miss Harrison, sister to Mr Harrison of the Treasury, and William Harrison the Barrister. I recollect once being acquainted with her, through my poor friend Murphy, who was Harrison's pupil and very intimate with the family so I accordingly made myself known to her and was recognised. Mr Veitch accompanied

us to the House of the Portuguese Governor of this place whose name is so long it would take the remainder of this sheet to write it, so that with your permission we'll let it alone till my return. From the Governor we proceeded to Brigadier General Meades, the Commander in Chief of the British forces here, for the Island is garrisoned by the 11th Regt. of Foot.

The General received us very politely and invited us all to dine with him the next day. On our return from thence I walked up to Mr Knox's house, which is on the outskirts of the town, commanding a pretty view of the Roads of Funchall and the Sea beyond. Mr Knox was unluckily gone to explore the Country, but Mrs Knox was at home and I had the pleasure of seeing her. She was extremely glad to see me indeed but very much surprised as she had not, nor had Mr Knox, the smallest idea of my leaving England. The probability of my obtaining my present situation never having being hinted to them. I had therefore to explain my own situation to Mrs Knox, which I hoped to have been saved and he gave us a most cordial invitation to come when we liked. I promised to bring Eliza and my little boy to dinner the next day, as I was going to the Commander's in Chief.

Colonel Macquarie and I fetched the Ladies from the ship to the Consul's house dined that day. There were several persons there, principally Captains of King's ships and passengers to the West Indies. Their Dinners are exactly the same as in England. But the meat is not so good indeed it is very bad and is usually stewed. But their poultry and vegetables and Soups are excellent. On Tuesday we had a Gentleman's party at General Meade's who is a very polite and pleasant man. He married a Miss Ann Dolling, a Daughter of the late Sir John Dolling. We dined very late indeed, not sooner than 8 o'clock – it is much the fashion in Madeira for the English to dine at a very late Hour – never before Six and at this house it is generally before Seven o'clock that we sit down. In the morning we called at Mr Knox's with Dr Shuter and while we were there Mr Knox returned home. I introduced Eliza, who was very kindly received and made to stay Dinner… Wednesday, Eliza and myself up to Mr Page's on the Mountain.

... Mr Plummer had given me letters to Phelps, Page etc. which I had presented and had ordered some Wine from them. I had previously received a pressing invitation to pass the whole of my time there with my Wife and Servants which I had not been able to accept. But on Mr Page's invitation, I was induced to call at his Country House...We returned to Funchall with Mr and Mrs Page after partaking of an elegant Luncheon. I dined that day with a Mr Gambier a young Man who is Nephew to Lord Gambier and is a Partner in the first Wine Merchant House in this place. Eliza and myself and Mr Veitch went to see the Performance of some Gentlemen of the Place who had established an Amateur Theatre. The Play was John Bull, all the World was there and much entertained. The Heat, however was excessive, the Performance was not over till past 12o'clock. We had received an Invitation for a Supper and Dance to be given after the Play by some Gentlemen who had formed themselves into a Society which they call the Anti-Melancholick. All the Principal Persons in the Place were there, But Eliza was obliged to return to her Little Boy and I was so knocked up by my fagging ride and excessive heat we declined going. Yesterday, Thursday, it rained Mr Veitch had a large Party to Dinner viz the Commander in Chief and Mrs Meade and a great number of Officers.

We have an Invitation from Captain Curtis of the Majicienne Frigate for a dance and Supper on Board his ship on tomorrow but I do not think that we shall go. On Sunday, I understood we shall positively sail – our first Place of destination will be St Jago, one of the Cape de Verde Islands, where we are to stop and refresh the troops with Fruits, fresh Meat, poultry and fresh Water. We are to then to proceed to Rio for the same purpose. This last step has been determined upon, only, since we sailed from England. From Rio... the Cape and then to Port Jackson. In two days we shall be in the regular Trade Winds... 5-6 weeks to Rio, from thence regular Packets to England of which I shall avail myself.

To Jeffery June 17 1809.

The thing that most amused us on board Ship was to learn the mode of communication by Signals or Flags, which is reasonably curious and pretty. We used often to talk and enquire after each other's health by signal of three or four Miles distance. Different Combinations of Colours formed different figures, and the combination of figures forms the Words. That is called the Telegraph. There is another in which different combinations of Flags form different sentences, which mode is used to communicate in action, and when the different Flags are surmounted by a Yellow Flag, it is meant for the Convoy.

… In the hurry of leaving Poor old England I forgot to procure any short sighted glasses and set sail with only one pair of spectacles and an eye glass, which latter is broken. I will thank you to send me by the next ship about a dozen glasses No. 9 in strong gold frame with a Pebble in it …

I assure you My Dearest Jeffery I never took anything to heart so much as the failure of Clarke's House not on my own account but yours.

I shall not send you any commissions but what are absolutely necessary, and I beg you will act on them according to your own Judgements and assure yourself that whatever you do I shall be satisfied. Two things I would wish to impress upon yourself and my Friends, first that you acknowledge the date of my letters and the conveyance if you can. I refer also to the dates of such of your letters as you are not certain have come to my hands and next that you repeat in several letters anything that you consider important or material. I shall set you the exempt punctually. I will thank you to tell my Dear Friend Harry (whom God bless) that since I wrote to him which I do by the same conveyance viz last night that Captain Pritchard had informed me that young P– had in the course of the day absconded from his Ship, had sold his own clothes, stolen from another Person and that tho' the English Consul had given orders to have searched for, he had not been found. I am sorry to communicate News which may distress his Parents but such is the Case. If any further transpires I will let him know at the first opportunity.

Mr and Mrs Knox have shewn Eliza and myself the utmost Kindness and attention and seem to like Eliza very much. She sang for them and they were both charmed with her voice … George Knox has given me two letters of Introduction, one to Mr Staples, his wife's cousin, at Rio de Janeiro, and another to Mr Alexander, Secretary to Lord Caledon[1] at the Cape. I hope he won't remember Aylesbury. He has also procured me one from Mr Gambier here (a partner in the House of one of the first Wine Merchants here) to his Uncle or brother, Sir James Gambier, Consul General to Rio Janeiro, which will be very useful for me. Last night Eliza, myself and a large Party, went to a dance given by Captain Curtis on board his Frigate the Majicienne. Everything was well managed and I was happy to see Eliza pleased. She danced remarkably well and is very fond of the amusement. The Quarter Deck was covered with Awnings, the Quarter a sides enclosed by Flags of the different Nations and in other respects it was fitted up as a Garden. The Band of the 11th Regiment played. We danced a great many couples and at 12 o'clock sat down to an elegant Supper in the Captain's two Cabins which were thrown open and made very Commodious. We did not leave the ship until Daylight.

Endnote

1   Alexander Du Pre, 2nd Earl of Caledon, the first Governor of the Cape of Good Hope after the English reconquest of the Cape in 1806. He consistently struggled with the Commander in Chief at the Cape, General Sir Henry Grey, and was to resign because of this in 1811. Bent is worried here because his father's fellow candidate in the Aylesbury election was a member of the same family, James Du Pre. A Biographical Peerage of Ireland, Nichols and Co, London 1817.

5

Journal from Madeira to Porto Praya

Monday June 19th

After a weeks stay at Madeira, by which we were much refreshed, at 1pm this day we once more embarked and very soon left the Town of Funchal behind us. I took leave of my Friends the Knox's with much regret, we had received from them every kindness and attention. Dr Shuter accompanied us to the landing place, where we took a long farewell. This day my Eyes were bad with a Moderate Ophthalmia, very prevalent on board Ship and from which neither Eliza nor the Servants escaped. It was accompanied with much pain especially on attempting either to write or read. Eliza was not without her sufferings, also, she was much distressed by the toothache.

Tuesday June 20th

The Breezes having been light and baffling during the night Madeira was very perceptible this morning. The day was very hot especially in the Sun – but as the Awning was spread entirely over the Quarter deck we did not feel much inconvenience from it. My Eyes were much better but Eliza's Face was very bad.

Wednesday June 21st

Our Progress in the last 24 hours has been but inconsiderable. During the Day we were sent in chase of strange Sail steering ahead of us. In a few hours we neared her and gave her a Shot, which instantly made her lower her Main Royal bring to and hoist her Portuguese colours. She was from Oporto loaded with Wine and bound to Rio Janeiro. She gave us no news. My Eyes were this day nearly well. But poor Eliza suffered much from the toothache.

Thursday June 22nd

On rising this morning I had a distant and fine view of the Island of Palma, one of the Canaries to the north east about 18 miles. The Land is remarkably high and rugged. By the assistance of good glasses we saw a quantity of Wood upon the Mountains. At 9am a strange Sail discovered from the Mast Head, bearing right before the Wind. Set all Sail and chased by Signal from the Commodore. We entertained hopes of seeing the Pike of Teneriffe but unfortunately, it was too hazy. At 3pm saw the Island of Ferro, the most westerly of the Canaries, at 4 came up with the chase, fired a Gun and brought her to. She proved to be a poor little brig from Madeira bound to St Antonio, one of the Cape de Verdes with Wine. At about 1am, a soldier having died, at Noon he was buried in the deep myself performing the Service at the request of the Governor … I forgot to observe that on Wednesday we had danced in the Evening but the Ladies did not take any part in the amusement. This evening respect to the poor Soldier whom we buried in the morning prevented any dancing. In the night we passed Ferro.

Friday June 23rd

At Daybreak came up and boarded a Spanish Brig bound from Malaya to Vera Cruz in South America with Wine and Spirits. She brought us no news. Our Commodore's anxiety to make Prizes must have subjected him to disappointment. We were all of Opinion that he was too solicitous to cruise and the main object of the Voyage the Conveyance of the troops with all possible dispatch was sometimes overlooked. It was said his reason for touching at St Jago was founded on the hopes of meeting with two Danish East Indiamen who usually stop at that place at this season of the Year. Our Winds were very favourable and their Regularity had the appearance of Trade Winds. But the *Hindostan* was a Mill Stone about our Necks and caused the most astonishing and mortifying delay. Even the Transport kept up with her under three Top Sails. I this day examined my packages in the Store room, in consequence of Colonel Macquarie having sustained much damage in his. I found one packing case containing several smaller cases, tore in pieces and very wet. My Tea Caddy was much rubbed and defaced but not broken, another containing my Gown was damp, and the Gown much spotted, but not so as to be spoiled. I also opened the Case containing my Shoes and Boots and found them all in good order, but gave Directions for them to be opened and aired and rubbed very well. In the evening we had a dance on the Quarter Deck in which the Ladies joined, but in consequence of the Officers having danced with the Soldiers' Wives in the preceding evening,[1] the Women refused to dance with the Soldiers.

Saturday June 24th

The Night was very fine and at Noon this day we were in Lat 25 1' N not more than one Degree and thirty Miles to the north of the Tropic of Cancer, which we therefore hope to cross tomorrow. This morning Bonetas, flying fish, and Dolphins were playing in considerable numbers about the Ship, but we did not succeed in striking any of them. The Heat is considerable, as the Sun is nearly vertical, but it is a little moderated by a refreshing Breeze and the shelter of the Awning. It is a singular thing to me to stand in the sun and throw no Shadow. In the evening we had a pleasant Dance on the Quarter Deck.

Sunday June 25th

This was the first Sunday during our Voyage that we have been able to have Prayers read Publicly on board Ship. This morning as the Weather permitted, I read them and the Quarter Deck was well fitted up for that purpose. All the Chairs were produced for the accommodation of the Ladies and Officers and a number of Chests were brought up for the Soldiers and Seamen. The Chair used for drawing the Ladies into the ship with a little management made a very good reading Desk and was placed immediately before the Binnacle, and the Sides of the Quarter Deck were enclosed with the Ensigns of different nations. The Audience were remarkably attentive. I was very busy today in my clerical Department, for after Services, I churched a Woman and christened a child. In the morning I saw a great number of Flying Fish – but did not observe any Dolphins. For two mornings past my little Boy has been ducked in a large Tub of Salt Water, and today I bathed him myself giving him two ducks, he liked it very much laughing in my face between each Dip. At Noon, our situation was in Lat 22.58' N Long 20 05' W. Sal Isle (one of the Cape de Verdes) bearing S 23 W distant 138 leagues, having run 27 miles since Noon yesterday. Our course is marked off each day on the Chart, so that we can at any time see the course we have steered and the distance we have run on any particular day. Altho' we have now crossed the tropic of Cancer and are in the Torrid Zone, with a vertical sun, we are not at all incommoded by the heat, which is very much tempered by the freshness of the Trade Winds, we again feel anxiety to see land and hope to see Porto Praya or St Jago by Wednesday… we shall have been in a few months in every Quarter of the Globe, endeavouring to find that, which those who have it set little value upon and squander away the means of supporting. I mean Independence, let me but once have thee in my Grasp and it shall not be my fault if I do not hold thee fast.

Monday June 26th

We are now got into the north east Trade Winds, which blew all last night very fresh accompanied with a heavy Swell of the Sea, which as we were sailing south west made the ship roll a great deal, but this we did not care about, as we knew we were making good Progress; accordingly at Noon this day, we found we had run in the last 24 hours 179 miles, being the longest run we have had since we left England. At noon we were in Lat 20, 13' N Long. 20 47 W Sal Isle bearing S 31 W distant 241 Miles and having reasonable hopes of reaching Praya Bay in good time on Wednesday. In the evening unfortunately, the Wind dropped a good deal and towards midnight fell entirely away. We had dancing on the Quarter Deck, but as there was considerable swell the Ladies declined joining. I must confess our Evenings are very dull, politeness prevents us from reading[2] and something or other always prevents us from talking or playing at Cards. We this day discovered another little bit of tooth peeping out of my little Boy's under gums close to the first.

Tuesday June 27th

A very quiet night, and a sound sleep, compensated for a want of rest on the preceding night but we had not made any great progress. At noon, we were in Lat 18 N and Long 21. 23' W Sal Isle bearing south west 113 Miles having run 128 miles in the last 24 hours. The Wind was still very moderate and we gave up all hopes of reaching St Jago before Thursday and confined our wishes to not being imprisoned by Calms among the Islands. In the afternoon, the Breeze freshened a little and at 7 o'clock the Commodore bore up with all sail set sailing so close under our stern and Spoke us. She desired us to make Sail in the morning for Land. It was a most beautiful Sight, the Majesty, the Grandeur, and the Ease with which so immense a body appeared to move through the Water, could not be exceeded. We were happy to hear that they were all well. In our own Ship very few were on the Sick List and those few owing to their own imprudence at Madeira. We have an extraordinary case of a woman, who by washing exposed herself to the heat of the Sun so much, while at Madeira, that she now lies dangerously ill, being scorched from the top of her head, all down her back which is one complete Blister. She is in a perpetual state of delirium. We have also some Men in Fevers from indulging too much in the Wine of Madeira.

Wednesday June 28th

Although the Morning was very hazy at 6 am the man at the Mast Head cheered us by the cry of Land, which proved to be the Isle Sal bearing W 33 Miles from us. Part of this land is considerably high, and may be seen in clear weather at an immense Distance. Our time keeper proves to be very correct, and enables us to find the Longitude with great accuracy, so that we made the Land exactly at the time we expected. Is it not wonderful, that after traversing the ocean, night and Day apparently without a Guide, and without seeing anything but Sea and Sky, we should be able to make with such precision, what appears as a Speck. It never before struck me so forcibly. After making the signal to the Commodore that we saw Land, we hove away and at 10 o'clock came within sight of the Island of Bona Vista, the land of which is very high. As we neared it we easily discovered its white Rocks and Cliffs, which put one in mind of dear England. The outline of this Land is remarkably strong and bold, presenting to our view some very high mountains and abrupt bluff cliffs. We shortened Sail, to enable the Commodore to keep up with us. In the Evening we had dancing as usual which is most excellent thing for the Soldiers and Sailors, who live so much on salt meat, as it is a great preventative of Scurvy.

Thursday June 29th

Early in the morning we made the Island of May or Mayo and at 10 o'clock it bore north west distant 9 miles. The appearance of all these Islands from the Sea is Grand and Picturesque, but barren. During the night a poor little flying fish, fatigued by flying from its enemy the Dolphin dropped into the Ship. It was the first I had an opportunity of examining from the top of its Head to that of its tail was 9 inches, from the tip of one wing to that of the other when stretched 9 inches. The Wings grow from the shoulder in the same manner as those of Birds. When wet they are easily expanded and enable the animal to fly, but they soon dry and then it must fall. Their utmost flight is nearly half a mile. The Dolphin pursues and catches them exactly as they drop, and sometimes they will make a leap at them of some feet out of the water. St Jago in sight. High land 25 miles distant, but the morning is rather hazy. At half after three o'clock, We cast anchor in Praya Bay, and at six we went on shore.

Endnotes

1 Soldier's wives were far inferior.
2 Perhaps because the others had no books or no-one was asked to read aloud. For a discussion of the manners surrounding reading see D. Selwyn, *Jane Austen and Leisure,* Hambledon Press, London, 1999.

6

Sketch of Porto Praya in the Island St Jago

June 29th 1809

I shall endeavour to give you some idea of Porto Praya, and of the Impressions it made on my Mind.

Porto Praya is the name of the principal Harbour in the Island of St Jago, one of the largest of a cluster of Islands, in the South Atlantick Ocean, which bear the name of the Cape de Verde Islands, from a Cape of the same name on the Western Coast of Africa, from which they are distant about 300 miles. The appearance of all these Islands from the sea is of the same character; and generally presenting to the view, high and fantastick Mountains and little appearance of fertility.

St Jago, though not the largest, is the principal, as it is the Residence of the Portuguese Viceroy, whose situation and circumstances do very little credit to so grand a title. Porto Praya, a Miserable Village, or rather collection of wretched Huts and the Immediate seat of Government, is the best Harbour in the Island and is situated on the south west part of it, in the 1415' 30" N latitude and Longitude 23 30' 17" W . The Bay, though very small, affords tolerably secure anchorage for shipping, at a very small distance from the Beach and appears very capable of defence. On one side of it is a small island called the Island of Quails, which has a very barren appearance, is separated from St Jago by a very narrow channel, and is defended by a Battery mounting 15 large Cannon.

Opposite to the Island of Quails, there is a high rocky point, defended by a battery of 7-8 guns forming the south west entrance of the Bay. The other Entrance of the Bay equally bold and prominent mounts a Battery of 15 guns. The Beach and anchoring Ground is a deep, soft Sand, but landing is rendered rather difficult by a heavy surf, which as the Bay is quite open to the sea, rolls at times with much violence.

The Village of Porto Praya stands upon high Ground, above the Beach, and the access to it is by very steep though not very long ascent, which leads to the Gates at which a Sentry is constantly posted. The appearance of the Country for some miles round it is by no means prepossessing; bearing few marks of fertility and consisting of a deep sand, which powerfully reflects in the hot season, the Rays of the Sun. The Climate is here very hot, as the Sun is vertical here, as in all places between the tropicks, twice every year. In the rainy season it is very unhealthy, especially in the Interior, and the Inhabitants suffer much from agues, fevers and liver complaints.

Though the eye is not gratified at Porto Praya by much verdure, yet as novelty is always interesting to the human mind, it is not wanting in objects to arrest the attention of a stranger. The fantastic shapes of the Mountains, the singular and novel appearance of the Palm Trees here and there scattered over the sand, the Cocoa Nut Tree, and several other Trees exclusively belonging to a tropical Climate, all make a certain impression on the Mind. But though the vicinity of Porto Praya is very unproductive, the Interior of the Island must be very much the contrary. The Soil in those parts, is very fertile producing with little or no cultivation excellent Pines, bananas, plantains, cocoa nuts, yams, guavas and abundance of other tropical fruits. There also may be had in greater abundance, poultry, Turkeys, hogs etc. As for Guinea Fowls they are innumerable, flying about wild, close to the Village, and may be had in any quantity, only for the trouble of shooting them. Indian Corn is here of course, in great plenty. Though I had no time to go up into the Country I know these things to be plentiful from the price they bear. We bought very fine and fat Fowls for 1/- each, most beautiful large Turkies for 5/- Pine Apples even to us, not more than 6d, which we have every reason to believe was 5d too much and everything else in proportion. Bullocks also are plentiful here, as well Sheep and Goats. Indeed this is an excellent place for procuring all kinds of Stock, when a ship can stay three or four days, so as to give the Natives time to drive them from the Country, and could we have remained that time we should certainly have been still better provided and at a cheaper rate.

The town of St Jago lies about three leagues from Porto Praya, in the interior, but as it is considered as rather unhealthy, the Viceroy resides at the latter place. Of this town I know nothing; but if it be not better than Praya, It is worse than the most miserable village in England. The

Town, if Town it may be called, stands upon high ground and consists of something like two Squares of miserable, low, stinking Huts, made of Mud and Plaister, few of them having Windows. Indeed I am informed they are very little better than the Negroes on the Coast of Africa. The residence of the Governor is more like a house, as it has two stories [storeys] and glass windows but they are such as would disgrace a tradesmen of the meanest village in England.

On the Evening of our arrival at Porto Praya, Captain Pascoe (our Commodore) and his wife, Captain Pritchard, Captain Birch and his wife, Eliza and myself waited upon the Governor and were received by his Aide de Camp (a Negro Officer who had previously very humbly solicited that his wife might have the honour of washing for us) into the Governor's Audience Room which was enough to make a Judge laugh. The audience Room of this Viceroy, who, bye the bye, is as ceremonious as any Monarch, is not a bit better and somewhat resembling what you in England call a Cockloft. It is literally a Garret, with the Headbreakers[1], etc. and serves his Excellency for Breakfast Room, dining Room, sitting Room and Audience Room, or as the song of the poor Cobbler says, 'for Parlour, for Kitchen and Hall'. It has no carpet, the want of which the heat of the Climate may well excuse, and the dirt of the plaistered walls is concealed partly by a Dozen Pictures representing the Crucifixion and the very Ditto of those hawked about by the Jews in St Paul's Church yard, and partly by two small narrow English Looking Glasses in gaudy Frames, the tops of which are bedizened with Suns and Moons and Stones in right Monmouth Street stile. The chairs and tables are equally contemptible. Fancy this room filled with some Men, they call officers and Aide de Camps, that is Negroes, dressed in very coarse Uniforms of Blue twined up with Red, and large, cocked Hats, or rather sundry pieces of old Hats of different shades from black to brown, clumsily sewed together in the shape of a cocked Hat, ugly as possible and stinking like Polecats, and you will have a tolerable idea of this Portuguese Viceroy's audience room and his Suite. In one corner of this Room is a Door opening on a few stairs, which descend into a place which is the Governor's Bed Room, his Study and private Audience Room. His Excellency did not see us that night; therefore after wandering about, till dark…we all made our retreat, which by no means any easy one, for as this Bay is open to the Sea, a strong surf beats on the Beach, which made it dangerous for Boats in the Dark. We were therefore obliged to follow, a very difficult unpleasant descent to some rocks where the Boat was sheltered, and over which the Sea beat with amazing violence. The Ladies were carried into the Boat, and the Gentlemen scrambled as they could, and without any accident we regained our Ship.

[The next day] we found [the Governor] at Breakfast in the Room I have before described and we were rather surprized in observing that he was so much more respectable in his appearance than we had fancied from that of his attendants, and his Residence. He is certainly the best of the Bunch and no Negro, but a portly looking well conditioned Portuguese. He was decently dressed, in a Scarlet Uniform and wore the star of some Military Order on the Breast. He is a married man, but in his Wife's absence (who, however, was daily expected,) he consoles himself in the Society of a fat, vulgar, Cornish Girl, who left England an Officer's Mistress, but now occupies the eligible situation of chere amies,[2] to this famous Viceroy. As the Governor does not speak English and has but an Imperfect knowledge of the French, the Conversation we had though short was tedious and was rather impeded than promoted by the clumsy efforts of a Negro Interpreter. But though I have been much amused by the Viceroy's Palace and Suite, I was still more entertained by seeing the Garrison parade.–

About 7 o'clock we were summoned by a Drum to this most extraordinary Sight. As this is the most exposed place, and is besides, the Seat of Government. I suppose it is defended by *picked* troops. They all consist of Negroes or Creoles, of a very black cast; and they are not allowed cloathing by the Portuguese Government, they bear a striking resemblance – and I am doing them much honour by the comparison – to Falstaff's ragged Regiment. There was not the most remote attempt at an Uniform. Some had Breeches, some trowsers and some neither, some had pieces of shirts, some bits of old waistcoats; button none, nor could I find a stocking. As for the arms of this Soldiery, they were of a pitch with their dress. Their Musquets were for the most part rusty, and broken and all of them without locks. In short, such a set of non effectives I never saw. Before they were dismissed they all began to chant what they called a Hymn to the Virgin; and made such hideous noises and grimaces, turning up their heads to the Sky and each trying to bellow louder than the other, that I began to think myself among wild beasts. Such dissonance never before assailed my ears.

While I am upon the subject of these Soldiers, I will relate to you a little disturbance which arose this day between them and the English. The Governor has a right here to levy a certain Tax on all Bullocks, sheep, monkeys, goats calves etc. that are intended to be taken out of the Island, no person therefore to take them out of the Gates, before that Duty is paid. A young Officer of the 73rd, not aware of this and taking stock out with him was opposed in a very rude manner by the Sentry, whom he jestingly threatened to run through the body, if he attempted to stop him. Thereupon the Sentry called out to his Commanding officer; who being a fellow half Portuguese, half Negro, took up the matter very warmly and earnestly. At this moment, the first Lieutenant of the *Hindostan*, came up, and told the Portuguese officer, if he behaved in that manner to an Englishman, he would capsise him. The Portuguese ordered him to be arrested, the Lieutenant drew his Sword, and swore he would put an end to any black rascals, that put a Finger on him. The Noise increased, the Negroes crowded round. A loud cry was heard of 'more English' all traffick was stopped. The Ladies screamed, swords were drawn, and the Drum was beat to arms.

I hastened with some Officers, to the Spot and found it 'confusion worse confounded'. The Gates were shut and the famous Troops assembled – and for a time we were all prisoners. Nothing could exceed the passion of the Portuguese Officer, or the ludicrous manner in which it was expressed. From not knowing English he could not tell how to give vent to his rage, so as to be understood by us; All he could do or say was to stamp and cryout, Tam, Tam, got Tam, me no speak English, why me no speak English. Both proceeded to complain to the Governor, who wisely refused to hear either, and ordered the Gates to be opened, the troops to be dismissed and the English to follow their business without molestation. Thus ended this notable Row.

Towards Noon the Country People came in from the interior, driving before them their asses, loaded with Skins, filled with Pines, bananas, cocoa Nuts, Guavas, Lemons of a beautiful mildness and other vegetables of various kinds. Some drove before them Flocks of turkies, goats, kids and others brought Fowls. As, however, they did not come so fast as our wishes required, each was obliged to be on the lookout, and get what he wanted for himself before the asses could reach the crowd of purchasers. This produce as before mentioned was sold reasonably. Happy those who could now muster an old coat, hat, breeches, uniform, Sword or anything of that kind. They were here as good as money and their anxiety for anything of that sort beyond what you could conceive. One Man came up to me to know what I asked for an old Blue Coat I wore, offering me a fine Milch Goat and kid for it; and when I told him I did not sell the cloaths off my Back. He asked me if I would part with the Buttons. Another wanted to buy my Spectacles from my Nose. For an immense old fashioned Hat I had in London sometime ago and which would have been the Tip of Haut Gout[3] here, I am sure I could have got a bullock; such is their Avidity and their want. The people are almost entirely black, but they import a great number of slaves from the coast of Africa, whose order and appearance varies much from that of the half bred fellows. Both Men and Women appear in general very well made having like all Negroes, very good eyes and teeth though their faces have no great attraction. When advanced in years, the Climate, hard labour and long dirty habits, make the women very disgusting. Indeed the Bodies of all the Young and old men and women, emit so strong a smell, as to render impossible to remain near their persons, or in their Huts.

The boys, even when arrived at a decent age, all run about perfectly naked, and the Girls and Women have only a petticoat about the lower part of their Waists and exhibit the Rest of their beauties gratis, to all who will take the trouble of looking.

It is almost needless to add that there is nothing like an Inn only some few miserable Huts, where they sell a sour wine and pernicious ardent Spirit. The Natives however, allow you to enter their Huts at your Pleasure, and have all of them something or other to sell. The Hut to which we all resorted, to make our bargains, which indeed might be called Exchange was one belonging to a free Negro woman of some consequence here, called Maria, who had several Slaves, and whose Hut was neater than any we saw. She had, one daughter of 35, amazingly tall and thin, being in a deep decline, who sat in a Corner of the Room the whole day without speaking. Maria herself was old, but was a fine looking Woman seemingly clean, and certainly better dressed than any of them, and spoke English tolerably well. But the Stench even of Maria's House was beyond endurance, and almost made me sick. Portuguese is the language commonly spoken here, and English is very little understood, which makes it difficult for Strangers to conclude Bargains with them, in which they are very keen, and never hardly lower their first demand.

They have great numbers of very pretty, green Monkies, with black faces, and long ringed Tails, several of which I might have bought for a Dollar a piece. The Heat is here very great, and was particularly so, at this time when the Summer is almost at its height.

Endnotes

1　Low ceilinged with beams.
2　He perhaps means amie tres chere – 'dearest friend'.
3　'Taint of decay' – a play on words.

7

Journal – Porto Praya to Rio de Janeiro

Saturday July 1st

After a stay of little more than 24 hours at Porto Praya, at 6.30 pm we weighed anchor, and taking advantage of a moderate and favourable breeze, we left this Harbour, of which we were sufficiently tired, having experienced but little comfort on shore and very much heat, hurry and fatigue. The Captain laid in as stock 2 dozen fowls at about 1/- each, 20 Turkies at 5/- each, 5 goats at 7/- each for milking and about 6 kids for eating at 1.3d each, besides Cocoa Nuts, Pines, bananas and Lemons. The oranges and Grapes were not yet in season I bought 20 pines at 6d each, which was three times as much as I should have paid, had we waited another day, 20 cocoa nuts at less, and some lemons tamarinds and bananas for almost nothing. As the country immediately around Port Praya is very barren, receiving most of its fruits from the Interior and as our stay was so short we paid much more than we should have done.

The manner of getting the bullocks on board is rather curious, a strong cord tied around their horns, which is held by one or two boatmen so as to keep the animal's head above water; the Boat then rows off, and the poor bullock is made to swim after it for about a mile, till it reaches the Ship; when a strong rope being lashed about its Horns and Head, it is hoisted on board by a Tackle.

Sunday July 2nd

The weather still very hot and the Wind very light. We were very apprehensive of a calm. I read Prayers in publick this morning to all on board, which rather fatigued me as the Heat was very great. In the Morning we caught a small Shark, but it was cut up before I had an opportunity of seeing it and made a savoury breakfast to the Seamen who are all very fond of it. The Night very hot and not a breath of wind stirring.

Monday July 3rd Another Shark caught but immediately cut up before I saw it and given to the Seamen. It was quite young and rather less than the first, which was 5 feet long. Quite a calm. This morning a little child died. At about noon the Seamen took a beautiful Nautilus called by sailors a Portuguese Man of war on account of its resemblance to a Ship in full sail, but owing to some awkwardness, it escaped before it was brought on Deck. There is no mode of escaping from the painful Heat, but sitting still and employing myself in some quiet way. I usually therefore after writing my journal and other things read to Eliza while she is working, untill Dinnertime, and by that means sometimes forget that I am in the Torrid Zone. At 6pm the Body of the poor little Boy was consigned to the Deep, and I had the melancholy duty of reading the burial Service. This day at noon by Observation we were in Lat 11 42' N and in the Longitude of the Cape de Verdes... At Midnight the poor woman who suffered so much from the Heat of the Sun at Madeira died of the weakness and fever brought on by that means.

Tuesday July 4th

The Wind very light and weather very cloudy. At 11am much Rain accompanied with Thunder and lightening but very light and of short duration. Unfortunately the Captain's cow gives but very little Milk, which is of great inconvenience to little Ellis who is very fond of Bread and Milk, tho' not yet weaned. He seldom has recourse to his Mother, till the evening and is much attached to Elizabeth ... Yesterday at noon the thermometer stood at 79, in a Cabin with two Windows open, to windward and not exposed to the Sun. At Noon this day we were by account in Lat. 17 and Long 24 10 W. St Paul's bearing S 17 W and 4 leagues distant. The Thermometer at the same time stood at 81 in the shade. About 2 pm the Body of poor Mrs Murray was buried, and I read the Service over it. At Nighttime the Heat and Flies were very troublesome.

Wednesday July 5th

The Morning very fine, but hot. The Wind fair, but not much of it; and of that little, the Heaviness of the *Hindostan* prevented us from reaping much advantage: it was indeed provoking to be obliged to bear this Heat a month at least longer on her account; and very strange in the Admiralty to send so slow a sailing Ship on so long a Voyage, and with a Vessel of so different a description. At Noon we found we were in Lat 10, 16 N and that we had run only 79 miles in the last 24 hours. The Thermometer at noon this day was 79 in the shade. During our Dinner we were much surprised by a signal from the Commodore to reconnoitre if the strange Sail in Sight were an Enemy. We had no idea that a Strange Sail was in sight, but we soon observed a large Vessel bearing down on us, with all sail set. We hauled our Wind and soon made up with her. At 2 miles distance repeated the private Signal of the day which was not answered, We then hoisted our colours, but she did not hoist hers. We then made the Signal for an Enemy. All men went to their Quarters, and we prepared for Battle. Eliza was dreadfully alarmed and cried much. It was now nearly dark. When [in] Musquet Shot distance we gave a Shot right ahead of her; in two minutes another. The Vessel closed and ranged herself alongside of us, and the Captain gave orders to pour our broadside into her, when she continued to lower her Topsail and shewed us she was an American bound to Canton in China, laden with Dollars, wood and Lumber. After boarding her we made sail to join the Commodore. In the evening a good deal of lightening and a little wind.

Thursday July 6th

Morning hazy, wind foul and much Rain. Towards Noon it cleared up and became cooler. We had communication this morning by Boats with the Commodore. All well. At Noon our Lat was 9° 27 N – Long 24° W. At 10pm it was very squally and rained very much. It continued to rain all the Night with great violence and was rather rough.

Friday July 7th

The whole of the morning very rainy, about Noon it was a dead calm, the Ship not having steerage way. The motion of a ship in a calm is very unpleasant. For in the immense ocean between Africa and America there is always a considerable swell, which, when the Sails are flagging about for want of wind, heaves the Vessel from one side to the other in a very tiresome manner. In the Evening we had squally winds which were unfavourable to us. At Noon we were in Lat 8 44' N Longitude the same as the day before or rather to the Eastward of it.

Saturday July 8th

Still Squally and unpleasant, at one moment a fresh Breeze and in the very next instant, in the twinkling of an eye a dead calm, so that the vessel has not Steerage way. In consequence of the damp weather, we had this day a thorough cleaning, furniture removed and carpet taken up and Floor washed. This Employment occupied the whole morning. The Heat is very oppressive in consequence of the want of wind and the number of Flies immense. They are sure to drive away all sleep at Daybreak, we are at a loss for milk for the little Boy. The Captain's cow gives but little milk. This day Latitude 8, 34' North and Longitude the same as the day before or rather to the Eastward of it.

Sunday July 9th

Very fine morning but very hot and little Wind, Prayers read in Publick, and the Band sang Psalms. Eliza very bad with her tooth, but she had a resolution to let the Ship's Surgeon draw it, which he did very well. At 2 PM a Squall of wind and rain but favourable which is everything. We did not change our Longitude which till we cross the line is always 24 or 23W. As we are now running down our latitude which at Noon this day was Latitude 7 42' North.

Monday July 10th

In the course of the Night the Wind had dropped and this morning at Breakfast time there was very little of it indeed. At Noon the Wind changed and blew strong against us. Our passage from the Cape de Verdes to our present situation had indeed been as unpleasant and tedious as our passage from Madeira to Porto Praya had been agreeable. We had reason to expect that as we approached the line, the Trade Wind would leave us, and that we should be exposed to baffling winds and sudden calms, but we did not expect this kind of weather so soon. This day our Latitude was 6 58' N–

Tuesday July 11th

Wind still strong against us and obliged us to tack and retack. At Noon Lat 6 48' – having gained only 10 miles in 24 Hours.– We have indeed been unlucky since our departure from Port Praya especially as we had every reason to expect a favourable Trade Wind.

Wednesday July 12th

Wind fresh at south south east and Ship lay within three points of her course, which is south by west. Crew and soldiers very healthy. Latitude 6 34 N. So that altho' we had run many miles we had made but few in our course. Eliza expressing a wish for a cot for little Ellis, by Dinner time the Captain very kindly had one made which he gave to her and had it swung.

Thursday July 13th

Wind still Fresh or rather more to the Eastward and from the steadiness of the Breeze and squally Weather, previous to it the Captain imagined we had already got into the South East Trade Wind which is likely to take us to Rio. The Commodore who visited us this afternoon was of the same opinion. It is unusual to meet this South East Trade north of the line. Our Latitude was this day Lat 5 52' N. For these few nights past, we have usually had a Rubber of Whist at silver threepences, which somewhat relieves the dullness of the long Evenings. The Days and Nights are now nearly of equal length as we approach the Line.

Friday July 14th

Wind and Weather same as yesterday, but not so fresh. Weather very fine, but very hot. At 11am saw an immense number of Bonetas leaping out of the sea at great height, to their amusement and ours we could not come near enough to strike them. Our Latitude this day was Lat 4 40' North so that we had gained 72 Miles in the last 24 hours which is more than we have done for some days past.

Saturday July 15th

We now find that we have got into the South East Trade Wind, which is gradually becoming more favourable for us. Our Latitude was Lat. 3 35' N. Eliza has for some little time been getting thin and is very delicate, so that she was advised to wean little Ellis, who was a great drain upon her, at night. Mrs M who was solicitous for this measure very kindly offered one of her cabins for his Nurse and him to sleep in and the Captain has kindly ordered a nice little Cot to be made for him. We this day all dined in the Ward Room with the Officers, who gave us a very comfortable dinner. We played cards in the evening and passed the time very pleasantly.

Sunday July 16th

I read divine Service, and one of the Bishop of London's lectures on the Gospel of St Matthew. The audience was large and very attentive. Our Latitude today was Lat 2 25' N. We retired very early this evening as is the custom with us on Sundays.

Monday June 17th

The Breeze was very fine and cool and pleasant. Our Latitude at Noon was Lat 1 25 N. My little Boy was this day nine months old and after dinner we all drank his health in a Bumper. This night Poor Fellow, Eliza began to wean him, or as the Captain calls it, to stop his Grog. He took possession of his new Cot and Cabin, but the dear Boy was very restless. He could not sleep at all, nor forget his mother. Eliza was in consequence very uneasy and passed the night in Tears. He had however, plenty of milk. The Commodore by signal this day invited all our party to dine with him the following day,but none of us liked the idea of dining out of our Ship, for fear of accident and therefore we all declined the pleasure and invited the Commodore, Mrs Pascoe and Colonel O'Connell,[1] instead of going ourselves, to dine on Board the *Dromedary*, to which they agreed.

Tuesday July 18th

I was this morning up very early, almost before Daybreak in order to nurse my little Boy. Captain and Mrs Pascoe and the Lieutenant Governor dined with us this day. And as Sailors like a good dinner and to shew you, My dear Mother, that we can get them altho' upon the Equator, We gave them at the Top a very good Leg of boiled Pork, at the bottom a remarkably fine Turkey roasted, a couple of nice boiled Fowls an excellent Ham, a Pease Pudding pumkin tart which is with a little lemon juice an excellent substitute for Apples, a plum pudding and a Cranbury Tart – Cheshire Cheese and a nice fresh Sallad from our own Garden – to eat. To Drink we had bottled beer, and Porter, Port and Madeira and as a Desert, Pine Apples, bananas and a most delicate and wholesome fruit, and fresh Cocoa Nut. Let it be remembered that we were now almost on the Line, in the middle of the Atlantic Ocean. Unfortunately Mrs P brought her little boy of 2 years and 4 months old who upset my tooth powder on my carpet and hid everything that he could find. He is a fine but spoiled child, and a great nuisance I found him. My little boy had a quiet night indeed, and affords us every reason to believe that he will be easily and well weaned. About 12 pm when we were all sunk in sleep, we crossed the Equinoctial Line and entered the Southern Hemisphere in Longitude 25 15' N – by timekeeper. The Breeze was cool and pleasant all the Evening but our Progress was much impeded by a strong current which ran against us to the north west at the rate of 73 Miles in 24 hours.

Wednesday July 19th

In consequence of an order from the Commodore, no shaving or Ducking or other irregularities were allowed to take place in either of the ships,[2] much to our satisfaction. Indeed, except the Captain, our crew and Sea officers are so young that very few indeed have passed the line, which would have caused much disorder, had the usual norms were [so] observed. At Noon we were in Lat 0 25 S – weather fine cool, and all on board healthy. In the *Hindostan* I am sorry to say there are 70 ill of the Dysentery – but no desperate cases and all occurring in the last day or two. My little Boy is very well and has plenty of milk and eats heartily and Eliza is now much at ease respecting him. The Captain had the goodness to have made for us a large bathing Tub to fit in our Quarter Gallery which is a great convenience to us as it enables us to dip my little Ellis which we have been obliged to discontinue for want of a tub, the one which we had first used being applied to the use of the Soldiers Wives. We had dancing on the Quarter Deck but neither the Ladies nor the Officers joined. In the Evening Col. and Mrs Macquarie, Captain P and myself had a Rubber which we won.

Thursday, July 20th

My little Boy had a charming night, and is quite well. Eliza, I think is now quite at ease respecting him; he eats very heartily of bread and milk, arrowroot and occasionally Mutton Broth. This morning he was dipped in his new tub filled with sea water and Eliza and myself also bathed, I sat down and threw three buckets of water over me. At noon our Latitude was Lat 1 17 S – with a strong breeze at south east. In the evening I played a game of Chess with the Colonel and beat him, the Ladies had a Rubber of whist, with the Captain and Major Gordon. Little Ellis was very well and ate heartily.

Friday July 21st

My little boy had rather a restless night but did not cry much, as he had plenty of milk. As we were sailing across the South East Trade, which was blowing rather fresh, we had a heavy Sea. At Noon Our Latitude was Lat 2 25' S Long 28 40' N – Eliza … is advised to take Bark. In the evening She had a Rubber at Whist. Weather Squally and wind high. In consequence of which we did not attempt to recover two Hammocks which fell overboard.

Saturday July 22nd

My little Boy had again but a restless night, but did not cry much. He looks very healthy and well. Our Latitude this day at noon was Lat 3 27 S Long 30 3' W. The *Hindostan* I think sails worse than ever and I fear in the course which we are now obliged to steer, as she cannot keep to Windward, nor on that account as well as others carry much sail, that we shall be on the Coast of America before we have doubled Cape Roque. If so, God knows when we shall get to Rio …

Sunday July 23rd

I read this morning Divine Service in Publick, but the motion was so violent I could hardly stand and now can hardly write, on this account I did not read any Sermon. My little boy had a very good night and continues very well. He seems already to have forgotten the Breast. We made much better progress in the last 24 hours than we expected, having run about 100 miles S by W. At Noon we were in Lat 6 39' S Long 31 38' W – by Chronometer; but there is an extraordinary difference of 80 miles in the Longitude of the two ships, the *Hindostan* being by her timepiece that distance more to Westward.

Tuesday July 25th

My little boy had an excellent night. At Noon in Lat. 8 4' S and Long 32 21' W sailing in a very fair course, though according to Captain Pascoe's account we ought to see the coast of America tomorrow or next day, which we do not wish to see before we make Cape Rio. Sent a Boat on board the *Hindostan* with Mr Carter Surgeon of the 73rd Regt. who amputated the Leg of a poor Soldier lad in that Ship which had been jammed by a Cask of Water falling from the Scuttle Butt upon it owing I suppose to some carelessness. He bore it without a Groan and Mr C– left him reading. In the evening played a rubber in the Governor's cabin.

Wednesday July 26th

My little Boy had a very good night, and is doing very well indeed. At Noon Lat. 9 25' S Long 33 4' W to the Southward of Cape St Augustine almost. If Captain Pascoe's account of our Longitude were correct, we should certainly be in sight of America. His time piece must be wrong. This Evening I read in Mrs M's cabin three Acts of *The Provoked Husband* aloud,[3] to Colonel and Mrs M, Captain Pritchard and Eliza.

Thursday July 27th

My little Boy...had so far forgotten the Breast that he cried on being only put to it ... At Noon Lat 10 56' S Long 33 22' W. At 4pm we were all much surprized by a Signal from the Commodore to tack, some thought it was owing to the difference in Longitude. Some that the Idea of going to Rio Janeiro had been given up and that we were about to make the best of our way to the Cape. All were discontented. But about 6pm we were still more surprized by a Signal to retack which we gladly obeyed, but could hardly believe untill we saw the *Hindostan* had wore[4] ship. In the evening I finished *The Provoked Husband* as before and played a Rubber.

Friday July 28th

After a little trifling Wind yesterday we this morning had a fresh breeze and are steering longer. At Noon Lat 12 28 S Long 33 45' W. At 1.30 passed within hail of the Commodore who sent a Boat on board us which explained the reason for his manoeuvring yesterday. He had discovered a very bad leak in his after Hold and had tacked in order to stop it. We were all concerned to hear this at the commencement of so long a voyage, the Sick List had also increased having extended to some of his officers and all grieved that the poor lad who lost his leg on the 25th was now suffering under a locked Jaw with little hopes of his recovery. Captain Pascoe had expended all his fresh provisions by giving them to his Sick and we therefore sent him a Quarter of Mutton and six Fowls. On all these accounts He was obliged to sail for Rio where we expect to arrive Sunday Week. Thank God! All in this ship are very well and there is not the slightest symptom of Dysentery on board. In the evening played two Rubbers of Whist.

Saturday July 29th

Notwithstanding the Interruption of yesterday we make tolerable progress in the last 24 hours as this day at Noon we were in Latitude 14 1' S – Long

34 07 W having run about 93 miles. The weather is very fine and cool, the Thermometer at Noon during the last week never having been higher than 78 in a cabin not exposed to the Sun. We this day spoke the *Oxford* transport whom we have had under our Protection from England bound with Troops. She is a very nice Ship sails very well and has not had a sick Man on board. Excepting some good Hams I do not think we have had salt Meat during the Voyage, and have constantly had good Potatoes and excellent Water from two good Drip Stones. The Ships Water is now getting very black and stinking. We have always been allowed to wash with it in the Cabin Mess. Played backgammon in the evening in the Governor's Cabin with Mr Prode, a Lieutenant in the 73rd regt. lost three Gammons and won twelve hits. One of the Officers always dines with us, taking every day in rotation. I occasionally amuse myself with playing chess with Captain Kenny of the 73rd who plays remarkably well. We have played only 3 Games but I have lost all though they were hard fought. I have played a few games with the Governor, but I have always won.

Sunday July 30th

Weather fine and breeze steady – at 10.30 read Divine Service and one of Blairs Sermons, on the Character of Hazael. Audience very attentive. Rather tired. At Noon Lat 16 15' S and Long. 34, 22. W. After tea at Mrs M's request read one of the Bishop of London's Lectures on the Gospel of St Mathew in her cabin to herself, the Colonel, Eliza, the Captain and Major Gordon. Bed at 10.

Monday July 31st

Weather cloudy but Breeze steady at about 7.30 a Whale of some size was seen by several, spouting; but I was not one. This is the first that has been seen by us. Indeed those that have been in these Latitudes several times before are astonished at having seen so very few fish. As every Anecdote however trifling must be interesting among such sameness. I shall relate a circumstance which occupied our attention, this morning one of the little Monkies which had been brought by the Sailors from Port Praya, having concealed himself overnight in the Birth, where Col M's servants sleep and my servant took up his abode for the night in one of their Hammocks. In the Morning when George was shirting himself he jumped on his shoulder, and made hold to do there what no one else could do for him at this George conceived just indignation and proceeded to inflict corporal punishment upon the offender, which the poor Devil not approving made his escape out of the Port hole but it was out of the frying Pan into the Fire. For unluckily resting upon the board with which the Port Hole is stopped and was balanced on a Canon. It gave way and capsized the poor beast into the Water, where he soon perished. At Noon Lat 16 37 S Long 34 45' W being about 550 miles from Rio Janeiro, where we hope to anchor on Sunday. We are now steering south by west but as soon as we are South of the Shoals of Abrolhos between Lat 18 and 19 S we shall alter our course two points to the west. In the evening played two rubbers at whist. Towards night the wind freshened very much.

Tuesday August 1st

During the Night it blew hard ... at 10am chanced a strange sail, at 10.30 tacked, fired and brought her to. She was a small Portuguese Brig from Buenos Aries bound to St Salvador, with tallow and oil. She told us that the Governor of Buenos Aries had been removed and that Ferdinand the 7th was there acknowledged King of Spain; After our Boat was returned At 12 made sail after the Commodore.

Wednesday August 2nd

During the Night the wind blew very fresh indeed and about 7am one of those grand Squalls I have mentioned came on attended with much Rain. All morning very squally. At Noon we were in Latitude 20 20' S and Long 35 33' W. having ran 131 miles in the last 24 hours. It rained very much all the afternoon. In the Evening I read Fielding's *Farce of the Mock Doctor* to Mrs M etc. in her cabin. It is a very spirited translation of Moliere's ' Le Médecin, Malgré lui' we afterwards played a rubber.

Thursday August 3rd

… At 6am made sail per signal to examine a strange Sail steering west by south. We had a pretty breeze and smooth sea and the vessel went through the water 8 miles an hour without any apparent motion. At Noon in Lat 21 34' S and Long 37 04 W having ran 113 Miles. At one neared the Chace and fired a Shot astern of her; She hoisted the Portuguese colours, but still sailed on, fired another Shot pretty close to her which made her heave to. We then fired one more and that brought her down to us. At half past one boarded her when she proved to be a Portuguese brig from the Coast of Africa laden with 532 female Slaves all under the age of twenty for Rio Janeiro. She had lost 50 which the Master of her said was a small number as they generally expect to lose one half of them and added that when any one of them fell sick he instantly threw them overboard, to save the rest. At 2pm bore down for the Commodore who is now steering south west. At 7 PM passed within Hail of him when he told us his Sick list was increasing again – and that he expected to see Land tomorrow and ordered us to steer west by south in the morning to look out for it. In the evening Read Fielding's *Farce of the Intriguing Chambermaid* aloud in Mrs M's cabin and afterwards played two rubbers but we never exceeded silver threepences. A very fine starlight night and a pleasant Breeze not in Bed till past 11 o'clock.

Reading aloud

Excerpts from Fielding's plays that Ellis Bent read to Mrs Macquarie etc.

Mrs Modern:	*Hark, I hear my husband coming downstairs. Husband did I say? Sure, the wretch who sells his wife, deserves another name. But I must be civil to him while I despise him. (From The Provoked Husband.)*

Dorcas:	*And I tell you, you shall conform to my will and that I was not married to you to suffer your ill-humours.*
Gregory:	*O, the intolerable fatigue of matrimony! Aristotle never said a better thing in his life, than when he told us 'That a wife is no better than a devil'.*
Dorcas:	*When a lady, like me, condescends to agree*
	To let such a jackanape taste her,
	With what zeal and care should he worship the fair Who gives him
	– what's meat for his master
Gregory:	*you rose as good a virgin from me as you went to bed. (From The Mock Doctor).*

The Complete Works of Henry Fielding Esq. Volume 3, Frank Cass, London.

Friday August 4th

At 7am Commodore made signal to us that he saw Land but his confidence in his Time Keeper must have deceived him for the wind in a short time blew it, according to his calculation he was eighty miles to the westward of us. The Morning was very beautiful and we had a fine breeze. At 11am saw some beautiful Pintado Birds they appear to be of the size and shape of a Pigeon, the bodies and wings white with black circles upon them. They are often caught with a Hook and line, they are the first we have seen, saw a quantity of beautiful Sea Weed which shows we cannot be far from the Soundings. The colour of this weed is yellow, with pretty yellow leaves and berries of the same. We also saw several Grampas. At noon We hove to – heaved the lead, but could find no sounding with a line of 90 Fathoms. According to the Commodore's account we should be in soundings to see land as he is 70 Miles nearer it than we are. Our Latitude at Noon was Lat 22 31' South and Long 38, 53' W.– Distance in the last 24 Hours 108 Miles and 81 Miles from the nearest Land. We this day discovered that little Ellis had cut his eye tooth and that it was nearly through, to his Mother's great delight.

Saturday August 5th

… At 10 o'clock the soldiers were ordered to fire with ball. Accordingly a Studding Sail Boom was rigged out at the end of the Fore Yard Arm and a Target was lowered from it. The Soldiers stood at the Gangway and fired one after another by Companies. They fired very well, as a great many hit the Target and several the Bullseye. We were sorry today to find that our butter which has hitherto been excellent is getting very rancid. At Noon a boat from the *Oxford* came on board with Colonel Cox of the Artillery who is going out to the Cape as Commander in Chief of the Artillery. Captain Wallis and another Officer of the 21st Dragoons. The Colonel is a plain unaffected man and Captain Wallis pleasant and sensible. They dined with us. Whilst in the Boat one of the sailors knocked down an Albatross the first Bird of that kind we have seen that was flying near them with an oar, when brought to us. It was quite alive, it measured 7 feet 1 inch from the Tip of one wing to the tip of the other; its head, neck and belly were white; its Back and Wings of a dark colour, its Legs and feet strong and yellow, the latter webbed, its Beak 4 inches in length, strong and hooked and of a yellow colour, and its whole appearance very grand and formidable. The Albatrosses are very ferocious birds and have been known to attack a Man when swimming. This one is as near as large as those seen off the Cape of Good Hope. At Noon; Lat 22 37' S and Long 39 27' W Distance ran 32 miles and distance from Cape Frio 145 Miles. At 3pm sounded and found ground (Sand and Shells) at 130 fathoms we are about 50 miles from the nearest land on trying again we found Soundings in 95 Fathoms. After Dinner at 5.30 saw the Land, between Cape St Thorne and Cape Frio, 46 Days after leaving Madeira. Also saw several strange sail, made Signals by firing a Gun, and Rockets to speak Commodore, brought to and sent our Guests on Board the *Oxford*. Spoke Commodore and told him we saw Land. In the evening read *The Lying Valet* to Mrs M and played at Rubber.

Sunday August 6th

Saw Cape Frio Before Breakfast, distance 40 Miles, no Service today, had a fine Breeze during the day and at 4pm were abrest of Cape Frio and come up with the Brig we had spoken before from the Coast of Africa. At Nine lay to for the night.

Endnotes

1   Sir Maurice Charles Phillip O'Connell, the penniless younger son of Charles Phillip O'Connell, County Kerry, Ireland. Dependent on his kinsman, General Count Daniel O'Connell of the Irish Brigade in the French Army. Maurice became Captain in the French émigré forces serving on the French frontier under theDuke of Brunswick. In October 1794 after the Irish Brigade had been reconstituted in the British Army he was appointed Captain in Count O'Connell's 4th Regiment. In May 1800 he was appointed Captain in the 1st West India Regiment with which he served in Surinam, Grenada and Dominica. In January 1805 he was appointed brevet major and transferred to the 5th Regiment. He distinguished himself in Roseau in Dominica. In October 1806 he transferred to the 73rd Regiment of which he became Lieutenant Colonel in May 1809. Commissioned Lieut. Governor in January 1810 in New South Wales. On 8 May 1810 he married Mary Putland, Bligh's daughter. He was granted 2500 acres which he called Riverston. Mrs O'Connell still held Frogmore near Evan. *Australian Dictionary of Biography*, p. 294.

2   This is highly unusual. Officers paid in rum to avoid ducking. For the usual ceremony see Dening, op.cit., pp.77-80.

3   Reading aloud could serve many social purposes. One's choice of book was important, one's 'stile' even more so. Reading could be flirtatious (it required the listener to gaze upon the reader far more than would normally be socially acceptable), it could be a pointed comment on the listeners (one's choice of text and word emphasis was important) or it could be theatre, in which case it was invariably elevating. See Selwyn, op.cit., p.176.

4   A nautical term 'wear' means to bring a ship, to come about. The *Hindostan* was brought closer by this manoeuvre.

8

Journal at Rio

Monday August 7th

Rose at six and saw the Sugar Loaf off the entrance of the Harbour... very narrow. By order from the Commodore we took the lead and about 6 o'clock we entered into this most magnificent and wonderful harbour and shortly after anchored opposite the city of St Sebastian's on the left side of it.

Tuesday August 8th

The early part of the morning was unfortunately very rainy, but as it cleared up about Noon the Commodore, Captain, Governor and myself went on board the *Foundroyant* the Flag Ship of Admiral De Courcy to pay a visit to the Admiral, who is Commander in Chief on this station and he received us very politely and offered to accompany us to Lord Strangeford's[1] the Ambassador's. Admiral de Courcy is an Elderly Man, very easy and mild in his manner and very good tempered. He does not however appear to me to possess sufficient decision or activity for his Situation and I should think liable to be swayed too much by Opinion of others. He succeeded Sir Sidney Smith[2] with whom Lord Strangeford quarrelled on account of his interfering too much in the Diplomatic Department. His Lordship is not likely to quarrel with his Successor on that Score. His station is too idle and quiet to be lucrative. It lies entirely out of the way of his enemies Ships and Frigates, the Captains here are all anxious to be relieved. In case of a Spanish War, indeed the case would be altered, but at present the only employ of our Ships here is to make a nautical survey of the different Bays, Harbours, Rivers and Soundings on this Coast, which are but little known, for the Portuguese have sadly degenerated from the nautical Skill of their ancestors and are now the worst Navigators in the World. Indeed the present Situation of our affairs both with Spain and Portugal afford a most admirable opportunity of making an accurate Survey of the different parts of the Coast which may in future be of much advantage to England. Accordingly the different Ships on this station have been employed in the promotion of this object, and one H.M. Ship *Agamennon* has lately been lost off Maladonado, in making a survey of the River Plata. She was a very old Ship, and all her crew were saved.

Admiral de Courcy has with him his wife and daughter. Of the first I have not seen enough to form any opinion. She appears to be a plain sensible woman, the latter is rather pretty, pleasing girl about 18. The Admiral went on shore, and introduced us to Lord Strangeford. His Lordship is too much of a courtier, to be wanting in any mark of external civility. He told us he would settle with the Portuguese Minister, the <u>Important</u> affair of the time and method of introducing us to the Prince Regent and would write us the Result, which he remembered to forget for Ten Days. His Lordship appears to have one of the best houses in St Sebastian's, but the Room we saw was but shabbily furnished. He is quite a young Man, rather Handsome. He is remarkably quick, shrewd, sensible and well informed, but is supposed to be wanting in Judgement. He is eccentric, capricious, testy and Jealous of the smallest interference with him, or of the least appearance of neglect or want of the most punctilious respect to him. His Manners are very formal, and ceremonious. In conversation He can if he pleases be be very pleasant and he talks Portuguese with the greatest fluency and accuracy. He is much wanting in that Hospitality which should be the conspicuous feature of a British Ambassador, and apt to forget the attention due to the Natives of his own Country. His stile of living is mean and he is very unpopular.

Wednesday August 29th

A great many Visitors called this day, and prevented us going ashore, for finding that Lodgings were very extravagant and very wretched, we are all obliged to content ourselves with sleeping and living on board Ship. Among our visitors were the Admiral Captain Curzon of H.M.S *Elizabeth* 74 guns; Captain Schonberg of H.M.S. *President* 44; Captain Yeo, the Heir of Cayenne – which province he has lately taken from Victor Hugues the French Governor – of H.M. Ship *Confiance* he himself when Lieutenant cut out of the Bay of Rosas, and has lately been made Post unto her. He is indeed a very extraordinary Young Man, a singular instance of rapid rise in the Navy without interest; by mere personal Intrepedipity. He is a very popular Character here, Mr Jamison[3] and Mr Harris[4] paid their respects to us. The Former was Surgeon General of New South Wales, and the latter Surgeon of the New South Wales Corps, and both lately arrived in company with Colonel Johnston[5] and Mr McArthur[6] from that colony, being brought by those Gentlemen as witnesses for them in case of being brought to trial in England. Mr Jamison dined with us and gave us much satisfactory intelligence respecting the colony. But we alarmed him very much when we informed him of the light in which the late proceedings there were viewed by Government at home; and that the New Governor had orders to send his friend Colonel Johnston home under close arrest. Dr Jamison was one of those who signed the Paper, declaring the interference of the New South Wales Corps, and the Deposition of Governor Bligh to be necessary, and left us much agitated.

Thursday August 10th

We all went on shore today with the Ladies and amused ourselves with surveying the different parts of the City, with which we were much pleased. Today I met Sir J. Gambier[7] to whom I had a letter from his cousin at Madeira which I had previously sent to him as he resides more than three miles from the Town. Mr Macneil to whom I had been introduced on account of a letter I had for his partner, Mr Staples (absent at the Rio Plata) from Mr G Knox his cousin, was with me at the time and introduced us to Sir James and I in my turn, introduced Colonel and Mrs Macquarie. Sir James has as little the appearance of a Man of business, as can be conceived. He looks more like the Man of Fashion and Gaiety. He lives in great stile here and is very hospitable on both accounts he is of course much liked, he walked with us to the Public Gardens which is very beautifully situated contain many beautiful trees peculiar to this tropical Climate, but are very much neglected. He gave us all so pressing an invitation to dine at Botafogo his country Residence on the following day, that we could not decline it and particularly he would insist upon my little Boy, being one of the party as he has himself a Family of young Children. Dr Harris and Mr Davison, a Settler in New South Wales, and a Nephew of Sir Walter Farquhar dined with us on board Ship and shewed several drawings of Sydney and other places in the colony highly interesting to us.

Friday August 11th

The Morning proved very favourable to our proposed excursion to Botafogo, which we wished to visit in good time to have leisure to survey its beauties. At 1 o'clock Captain Curzon very kindly brought us his fourteen oared Barge. This Day was very hot. But the Awning which covered the whole boat was a great relief to us. The Row was very pleasant, and we had many fine Views of the Harbour, Islands and Shipping and though the distance was more than 6 miles the Sailors pulled us there in an hour. Sir James's House stands at the end of a small and beautiful Cove, on the Western Side of the Harbour called the Sugar Loaf and and is so surrounded with mountains as to have the appearance of a charming Lake to those who are at the extremity of it. Sir James Gambier ... has indeed a very excellent verandah, an open Room, at the part of the house which gives it I am told the appearance of the Houses in the East Indies. But at present, he is surrounded by Workmen of course the Confusion was too much to allow us to see the place with advantage. We were very hospitably received, and my little Boy was made much of and greatly admired . After having sat down a short time we sallied out to look at the prospect and the proposed improvements...The House is most elegantly furnished in the English Style and is much superior to anything in the Brazils not excepting, I believe, the Palace. His style of living is splendid and I am told uniformly so. Lady Gambier is a charming Woman, I suppose about 36. She is not handsome but very pleasing, is very affable and attentive, has great taste, and is, I am told, always the same. Her Sister, Miss Snell is a sensible accomplished woman and excels particularly in drawing. I should think her turned 30 some time, and she is not handsome, rather coarse and embonpoint.

Saturday August 12th

I went on shore with Eliza today, and after having walked about some time we returned on board much fatigued by the heat, to dinner.

Saturday August 13th

I read Divine Service this morning and one of Blair's Sermons on the Duty of the young in public. The Commodore was present. We all dined on board the Commodore's Ship. Captain and Mrs Pascoe are very unassuming good kind of people. He was Signal Lieutenant to Lord Nelson at the Battle of Trafalgar, and made the celebrated Signal; 'England expects every Man to do his Duty'. In the Morning, the *Magicienne* came into Port, commanded by your Friend Captain Curtis; and in the evening He surprised us all by a Visit on board the *Hindostan*. We were all glad to see him, as we felt interested in a fellow Voyager.

Monday August 14th

We all dined this day at Admiral De Courcy's. His House is in a small but pretty Island on the Eastern side of the Bay which abounds with all the Tropical fruits I have already mentioned. We met several naval Officers there and passed a pleasant day. His manner of living is unostentatious, differing much from the splendour of Sir James Gambier. His House is very small.

Wednesday August 16th

Went on shore and walked about the town a good deal, but returned soon after and passed the evening in writing letters.

Thursday August 17th

Sir James Gambier enlivened us all by giving us a very gay Ball at Botafogo. All the Ladies and many of the Officers of the 73rd were invited. Eliza and myself were engaged to dine at Mr Macneil's, whose habitation is near Sir James's. Captain Schonberg took us there together with Colonel O'Connell in his Boat. The House or Hut is quite small and not remarkable for either neatness or comfort. It is a Batchelor's Hut. However we had a good dinner. Though the rascally Portuguese Cook turned Sulky and made us wait for it, till past 7 o'clock. We met here several Naval Officers, amongst the rest – Captain Carter of H.M.S *Hyacinth*, brother of my old friend W.H. Carter of Peter House. I made myself known and we soon became intimate. During the rest of our stay, we received from him the greatest civilities and attention. He sent us about 8lbs of good tea and a Quantity of White Sugar Candy, a large bottle of real Indian Curry Powder, some eau de Luce, aromatic Vinegar etc etc. He had first come from St Helena. In the Evening Sir James Gambier sent down for us, the Swedish Envoy's carriage; the Ball went very well. The Band of the 73rd played. Lord Strangeford was there, the Papal Nuncio and many Portuguese. The only remarkable one was a young Lady, Sister to the Marquis de Bellas. She was a very extraordinary dresser. I wish I could describe her dress and danced extremely well, though in the operatic Style. She is said to have been deeply in love with Sir Sydney Smith, and to imitate him in the manner of wearing her hair. We had an elegant Supper, at which 60 sat down and did not reach the *Dromedary* until 4 o'clock am.

Friday 18th August and Saturday August the 19th

We did not rise till late and then went on shore to purchase necessaries for N.S. Wales. I bought 96lb weight of Sugar 87 of Coffee 32 of cocoa, 206 of Rice, and 65 Gallons of Brandy. I also have purchased a lamp for my Cabin, the want of which has been hitherto a great inconvenience to me.

Monday August 21st

Went on shore for a short time, but returned soon, as we were engaged to a dance on board the *Confiance*. But the Night proved very tempestous and we were obliged to give up all thoughts of attempting to go. All the ladies were invited and we were all much disappointed both on our own and Captain Yeo's account who had made great preparations for us.

Friday August 22nd

We went on shore and remained there some time to hurry the embarkation of our little Cargo and returned on board to dinner much fatigued. Dr Jamison dined with us and Mr Harris came in the evening and both took leave. He promised to see my Father the first moment after his arrival.

Wednesday August 23rd

At 6am we weighed anchor, taking advantage of the Land Wind, got out of the Harbour by 10 o'clock after having passed 15 days there very pleasantly. But it must be admitted that our longer stay would probably have been prejudicial to our Crew, who notwithstanding all precautions smuggled on board Quantities of a most pernicious spirit which was very injurious to them. The last morning we were obliged to flog 4 persons, one of whom was Coxswain of the Captain's Cutter, who with his Companions was detected in attempting to bring on board 8 gallons of this spirit in Bladders, which they concealed in the crown of their Hats.

Endnotes

1   Lord Strangeford, Percy Clinton Sydney Smythe, 6th Viscount, a diplomatist, born in London 31 August 1780, eldest son of the 5th Viscount. Percy graduated at Trinity College Dublin where he won the gold medal. In 1802 he entered the diplomatic service as secretary of the legation at Lisbon. In the following year he published *Poems from the Portuguese of Camoens with Remarks and Notes*, this was scathingly reviewed by the poet Byron but was reprinted several times. Strangeford became important in the Portuguese

court. In 1806 he was named minister plenipotentiary ad interim and he persuaded the Prince Regent of Portugal after the advance of the French in November 1807 to leave Portugal for Brazil. On 16 April 1808 he was appointed Envoy Extraordinary to the Portuguese in Brazil. *National Dictionary of Biography*, Macmillan, London, 1885, p. 603.

2   Sidney Smith was born into a Naval family with connections to the Pitt's. He joined the Navy in 1777 and fought in the American Revolutionary War. He served in the Swedish navy in 1790 and was mocked for this in England as the 'Swedish Knight'. He fought against France for the British. In 1807 Spain and France signed a treaty to divide Portugal between them and Smith was sent by London to assist the Portuguese, he arranged for the Portuguese fleet and Royal Family to sail to Rio de Janeiro. He was recalled to Britain in 1809 after planning with the Portuguese to attack Spanish colonies. E. Howard, *Memoirs of Admiral Sir Sidney Smith*, Richard Bentley, London, 1839. This writer disagrees with Bent concerning the quarrel, arguing that Smith and Strangeford disagreed only on the issue of diplomacy and were otherwise on good terms, Vol II, p. 127-65.

3   Thomas Jamison, baptised 17 February 1745, son of a rector. Educated at the University of Dublin. In 1777 he received a warrant as a naval surgeon and in 1786 was appointed surgeon mate of the Sirius, arriving in the First Fleet in January 1788. He was at Norfolk Island and Sydney, until September 1800 when he took 12 months' leave. He arrived in Sydney from England in June 1802 and was appointed acting surgeon general in Balmain's absence. In 1804 he, with Harris, carried out the first successful vaccination of children against smallpox. In 1805 he court-martialled two assistant surgeons, Mileham and Savage, for neglect of duty for refusing to attend a childbirth, but the War Office decided that these charges did not come under the Articles of War. This incident led to permission for surgeons to engage in private practice. Jamison was always distressed about the lack of medical supplies in the colony. In 1806 he sought leave to return to England to bring out his family. Governor Bligh refused permission until another assistant surgeon could be found. Bligh accused Jamison, along with John Macarthur and D'Arcy Wentworth, of becoming discontented when their trade in spirits was checked. Jamison supported Wentworth when the latter was court-martialled by Bligh, he gave evidence for Macarthur when he sued Robert Campbell Jr for trespass. He was among those who deposed Bligh in January 1808 and was appointed magistrate and naval officer by the rebel government. He sailed on the *Admiral Gambier* in 1809 to be witness for Johnston in the inquiries soon to be held in England. *Australian Dictionary of Biography*.

4   John Harris, born at Moneymore, County Londonderry, Ireland. He trained in medicine at the University of Edinburgh and was a surgeon in the navy in India for 10 years. In 1789 he was appointed surgeon's mate in the New South Wales Corp and he reached Port Jackson in the *Surprize* in June 1790. He was stationed at Parramatta. In December 1791, after the resignation of his superior, Harris was appointed to his place. In 1793 he received a 100 acre grant at Parramatta and he bought the farm of James Ruse. By 1800 he held 315 acres of land. In that year he was made a magistrate and put in charge of the police establishment. In 1801 he succeeded Surgeon Balmain as naval officer. He wanted to curb the liquor trade and was in conflict with his fellow officers. He reported conversations he had overheard concerning criticism of Governor King for favouring the visiting French and was consequently charged with ungentlemanly conduct. Six

months later he was court-martialled again for disclosing how two of his fellow officers had voted at a court martial over which he had presided. On both of these occasions he was acquitted but disbarred from public office. Feelings subsided by 1804 and he was reinstated as Naval Officer. In June he was resworn and made magistrate and controller of police in Sydney. Though he was friendly with King, Governor Bligh held a different attitude and dismissed him from his position. Harris became a bitter opponent of Bligh and espoused the cause of the officers in the Rum Rebellion. Major Johnston reinstated him as magistrate on 27 January 1808, but Harris was too critical of John Macarthur. In April 1808 Johnston dismissed him and ordered him to London to present the rebel cause to the government. Harris refused to go and in 1809 was appointed magistrate once more, he left for England three months later. *Australian Dictionary of Biography.*

5   George Johnston, born 19 March 1764 at Annandale, Dumfreishire, Scotland, son of Captain George Johnston aide-de-camp to Lord Percy, later Duke of Northumberland. A patron secured for the young Johnston a second lieutenancy in the 45th Company of Marines on 6 March 1776. He served in New York and Halifax in 1777-1778 and was promoted to first lieutenant and spent the next two years recruiting in England. In 1781 he embarked on H.M.S. *Sultan* and was wounded in English battles with the French in the East Indies. After six months' leave he sailed with the first fleet in the *Lady Penryn.* He was appointed brevet major in January 1800 and he quarrelled with King and Bligh. In 1800 he was sent to London under arrest for illegal trading in spirits, he was not brought to trial and returned to Sydney the next year. In 1804 he was key in crushing the Irish Rebellion. On 26 January 1808 he assumed the lieutenant Governorship and arrested Bligh. He returned to England where he was court-martialled in 1811, he was cashiered and returned to New South Wales. *Australian Dictionary of Biography.*

6   John Macarthur, baptised 3 September 1767 at Stoke Damerel near Plymouth, England, second son of 14 children born to two expatriate Scots. His father was a mercer and draper. John Macarthur obtained an ensign's commission in Fish's Corps which disbanded in 1783. Macarthur on half pay retired to a farm at Holsworthy in Devon. He obtained an ensignship in the 68th Regiment and in 1788 served in Gibraltar. In June 1789 he transferred as lieutenant to the New South Wales Corp. He arrived in New South Wales in 1790 where he acted as if he was superior to everyone else. He was appointed Regimental paymaster with added salary and was granted Elizabeth Farm in 1793, 100 acres. He became the foremost landholder in the colony selling his produce to the government. He argued with Governor Hunter and resigned as inspector for public works. He became active against Hunter, writing to England. He tried to enlist Paterson against Governor King and was subsequently challenged to a duel. He was arrested by King. Sent to England by court martial, on the voyage he managed to obtain powerful friends in each port. He returned in 1805 to New South Wales. Bligh rejected his pastoral schemes and imprisoned him without bail. Colonel Johnston intervened and deposed Bligh ordering Macarthur's release. Paterson allowed Macarthur to leave the colony along with other rebels who supported Johnston. *Australian Dictionary of Biography.*

7   James Gambier was appointed Consul General to Brazil in 1808 in the same year that Brazil's ports were opened to 'friendly nations'. He was, writes Gareth Atkins, part of appointments from the 'mercantile and pious' class to foreign service.He held office until 1814 when he was disgraced in diplomacy and recalled. He had massive debts

and was saved from bankruptcy by relatives and merchants, after which he became Consul General to the Netherlands. Bent excels at description here. See Gareth Atkins, *Wilberforce and his Milieux, the Worlds of Anglican Evangelicalism c1780–1830*, PDF Cambridge, online, 2007.

9

Account of the City of St Sebastian's and the Harbour of Rio Janeiro

In pursuance of my Original Plan I must now attempt to give you as accurate and amusing an account as I am able of the City of St Sebastian's, Rio Janeiro, the Capital of the Brazils and at present the seat of the Portuguese Government. But I must request you not to expect a very satisfactory account. For my stay was short, my time much occupied, and not being a Single man I had not that freedom of going about and that opportunity of seeing the different parts of the Country which those possess who have no persons but themselves to attend to. My Account must therefore be very superficial, and the Picture must derive all its interest from that interest, that is felt for the Delineation.

I shall first endeavour to give you an idea of the Harbour of Rio Janeiro, and the Situation of the City. next I shall describe the City itself, its appearance external and internal, its Inhabitants, public Buildings and amusements. I shall then give you some account of the Prince Regent and the Royal Family and his Government, then the different orders of his Subjects, the surrounding Country of its productions, and lastly such miscellaneous matter as I may have forgotten or not been able to arrange under the above Heads.

After having passed Cape Fino in Latitude 22 54 South you sail along a bold mountainous and highly picturesque shore, for about 120 miles (being all the while in Soundings) till you reach a Chasm which appears to have been formed by the preternal Separation of an Immense Rock of Granite. The Western side of which rising about 800 feet above the Level of the Sea in a very abrupt stile and assumes the Shape and bears the name of the Sugar Loaf. This Hill is esteemed inaccessible; and at any Rate no attempt has hitherto been made to scale it. Indeed when Sir Sydney Smith proposed to the Prince of Brazil to dig a Path to the Top of it and plant there a Battery of Cannon, the Portuguese Government were much alarmed at the proposal. For a Battery so situated would command every defence round St Sebastian's and if once in the possession of an enemy would be the means of reducing the city and Ports to surrender at discretion. The Portuguese therefore are very jealous of any attempt to reach the Top. The Eastern side or Check of this chasm is not near so abrupt as the Western check but still is Lofty and composed of a Rock exactly similar. The Sea entering between these two checks, which are about a Mile apart, suddenly expanding itself into a capacious Basin which runs into the Bosom of the country for many, many Miles, forms one of the most spacious, Magnificent and secure Harbours Imagination can conceive. In the centre of this chasm is a small island, and the passage between it and the Eastern Check which is about half a Mile in width, and bears the name of the Narrows, is the entrance into this Harbour, and through which the Longest Man of War in the British Navy may safely sail.

On all the Hills there are Batteries and Signal Posts, on every Island there is a work of annoyance and on the foot of the hill which bounds the eastern Entrance, there is a very strong and handsome Fort, commanding it in every direction, with three or four tier of Guns; so that if all the batteries and forts were properly manned and defended (which is never likely to be the case) St Sebastian's would be impregnable on the Sea Side by any Force that could be brought against it. And this is the Opinion of most of the Naval Officers here.

It is supposed to be badly defended at this time and to depend entirely upon our Fleet for protection, and the Ministry are exceedingly alarmed at the approach of any strange Sail. Lord Strangford informed us that they took the *Hindostan* and *Dromedary* for Two Line of Battle Ships, and our little Convoy for a Frigate, and were exceedingly alarmed and anxious. And the Prince would not be easy until Admiral de Coucy had sent a vessel to reconnoitre us.

From Cape Frio to Rio, every Mountain and Island are covered with Trees of the noblest appearance. The Harbour consists of so many Islands and is so large that it is hardly possible to see the mainland on the Eastern Side what appears to be the mainland being in part Islands. These Islands are remarkably picturesque, being high and Rocky, yet well wooded, and abounding in all the Tropical Fruits and trees which are filled with the little Humming Bird.

On the Western Side of the Harbour about 7 Miles from its Entrance, stands the city of St Sebastians and though its Site cannot be healthy, its appearance is certainly very Grand. It is built on low, swampy ground, between two high Hills, one of which entirely excludes it from the benefit of the Sea Breeze, which blows very regularly here from Midday until Sunset, and is wonderfully cool and pleasant. The Mountains about four Miles behind the town exclude it also from the Land Breeze. All these Hills are remarkably well wooded, those near the town being covered with the most beautiful Mangoe and Orange trees. About Sunset a thick and heavy Damp may be seen rising very high from the Swamp, and enveloping the town in its noxious Vapours accordingly Intermittent fevers and violent Agues are very prevalent here. The English Merchants here have all on this account Houses in the Country where they sleep. For though the town is unhealthy neither the Harbour nor the Country though the Heat is very great are liable to this reproach. On one of the Hills I have mentioned as being there is a convent on the opposite one there is a very handsome Monastery of Benedictine Friars, and the Episcopal Palace.

The Town lies between these two Hills, and the principal street (Rua Duetta) leads from the Prince's Palace which is near the Convent in a straight line to the Monastery. The first appearance of the Town is the better part only being visible which is a Square a few yards only from the Shore; two Sides of which are taken up by the palace, the Prince's Chapel, and the Episcopal Church. The third consists of some good private houses, and the fourth being open to the Sea; only containing a Fountain in the Middle, which is supplied with water by a very handsome Aquaduct, not far from the city which in its turn supplies the Shipping. The landing place is a convenient one, but though the harbour is almost landlocked, it is so capacious that there is almost always a considerable Surf, especially when the wind blows fresh from the sea.

One side of the Palace, but not the principal part, exactly faces the Beach and to see only this Side one should form but a mean idea of the building. But on advancing into the Square, and obtaining a view of the principal part which forms one Side of it, it assumes a really handsome appearance; though by no means grand, and displaying no architectural ornaments. It is a large, plain, oblong, whitewashed Building, the lower parts of which is principally occupied by a Piazza or Area for the Attendants or

Sentries to walk in during the rainy or very hot weather. Indeed as I have mentioned before in my Account of Madeira, the Portuguese never occupy the ground floor of their houses but always live on what we call the first floor and appropriate the former to menial or Commercial purposes. This Palace was the Residence of the late Viceroy, and since the arrival of the Prince has been enjoined by a building connecting it with the Prince's Chapel and Cathedral, to both of which he now has access without the necessity of going into the Square. The churches in the city are very handsome, and the Steeples, or rather Towers beautifully ornamented by Fret work and add extremely to the external appearance of it.

The Royal Chapel where the Prince and Family attend is remarkably handsome, indeed more splendid than anything of the kind...But notwithstanding the richness of this Chapel; it is surpassed by that of the Monastery I have mentioned, where all the ornaments were of pure Gold. This Monastery is at present the Residence of the papal Nuncio, a very fine old, Italian Nobleman of great Information elegant Manners and prepossessing Countenance universally esteemed by both Natives and Foreigners. It contains also 45 Benedictine Friars, and an excellent Library and from its elevated situation commands a most magnificent View of the town and Harbour and is supposed to be very healthy. The Principal Street is really very good and much handsomer than I expected to see. It is I should think a Mile in length and the width is by no means despicable. It contains many good shops, plentifully stocked with English Goods of all kinds. But those who expect to purchase them cheap in small Quantities will be much deceived. Indeed a Portuguese always charges a Foreigner, though settled in the place, three times as much as he does a Native, and generally abates as much of his first demand as a Jew. Chinese Silks and Indian Goods are also to be met with, cheap, in great abundance. In this Street which runs parallel with the Beach and very near it, the Custom House is situated; which is a large though not a handsome building, where much business is done: very slowly.

But the Street which most attracts the attention of strangers, is the Jewellers Street (Quandos Orivos) which is very long and consists entirely of Jewellers Shops. But the external appearance of these shops very much disappoints expectation. For they afford no glittering display of their goods arranged in an elaborate manner to attract attention and awaken desire. Just at the entrance there is a glazed cupboard carefully locked, containing a few gold sleeve buttons and tawdry Crosses; But their most valuable articles are within, locked up. They are extravagantly dear, and though they show you some beautiful Stones, Amethysts and Topazes especially, are very deficient in taste and [they] set them very badly.

... In the outskirts of the town, towards the south, there is a very beautiful and public Garden, which with English care might be rendered delightful. It is beautifully situated on the Sea Shore, and on that side of it, there is a handsome terraced Walk, which overlooks the whole Harbour and as you may well suppose commands lovely prospect. It contains a number of handsome Mangoe Trees, Oranges, Lemons etc and considering the general inattention of the Portuguese is tolerably clean and well taken care of.

The town itself of which I had a very good Bird's eye view from the Tower of the Churches, covers a good deal of ground and is very large. It is tolerably regular the Streets running parallel with each other, and being crossed by each other at right angles. Except in very fine Weather it is very dirty, for besides that it lies in a swamp. The streets have only a channel in the middle, to carry away the water and the Inhabitants have no idea of paving. Lord Strangeford told us he made an application to the Ministry to have the Street paved in which he resided, as it was really dangerous to drive a Cabriolet in it... for no persons of rank walk here. The Minister promised to do as he wished and the inspector actually came to Lord S– to obtain his Instructions about the London mode of doing these things, as Paving was an art utterly unknown in the Brazils.

The Heat of the town of St Sebastians must in the Summer Season be very great indeed. For although it was winter when we were there the Thermometer in the sun rose every day to 110 degrees. Near the Palace between the principal Street and the Beach is the principal Market, which is very plentifully supplied, with fruits, vegetables, Eggs and Fish. The place itself, however, is very dirty, and the Sellers are all Negroes. Little Negro Boys run about with baskets, like the basket women in Convent Garden and for the same purposes. Cabbages, Lettuce, Green Peas, Onions, Yams, Sweet Potatoes, oranges, Limes are in great plenty and cheap ... Fowls, Geese, Muscovy Ducks and Turkies are dearer, but very fine. And as for Fish, they have Mullet, Rock Cod, Snappers and the most delicious and largest Prawns I ever saw. But it is very dangerous to buy a strange Fish here, as many of them are highly noxious, if not poisonous.

Among these injurious Fish The Mackarel never fails to prove highly prejudicial to those who eat it. And many Englishmen, particularly sailors have fallen a sacrifice to it from Ignorance; for it perfectly resembles the Mackarel of our Coast in outward appearance. The Mackarel of N.S. Wales, by the bye, is I am told almost as prejudicial. The Population of this town is estimated at 40-50,000 Portuguese and Natives. Of the former 10,000 are supposed to have come with the Prince. In addition to these, there are thought to be at least 30,000 Slaves by whom almost all the manual labour of every kind is done. A small Island nearly opposite the town there is a very good Building appropriated to the use of the Navy here as a Hospital, and it is a very good one. To this almost all the sick on board the *Hindostan* were sent the Rest being sent on board a Transport. They received great benefit from this arrangement.

Having now mentioned what I recollect in regard to the Town itself I shall proceed to make a few Observations about the Inhabitants; dividing them into different Classes the Slaves, the Ladies, the Nobility, the Lower order, and the Royal Family. I shall first begin with the Fair Sex. Of the ladies here I am sorry I cannot write much to their advantage. But I must premise that this is the fault of a highly defective education. This is at all times neglected and is limited to their writing their own language and reading their Missal and attending to their dress. Their Minds and the formation of their characters and principles are utterly overlooked. Their employments are as trifling and uniform as their education is limited. Their time is occupied either in minute attention to the tedious ceremonies of their Religion, or to perpetual gazing out of their lattices (for very few houses in Rio have windows of glass) or riding about in their Palaquins, which it is their pride to have as magnificent as possible or to studying their Dress, which is gaudy and splendid to the last degree. Indeed, all ranks of females aim to make as much of their appearance as possible; and those who cannot afford ornaments of intrinsick value, bedizen themselves with Tinsel. Nothing that glitters, nothing that is gaudy, comes amiss. The Broadest Ribbands, the largest Earrings, the finest laces are the sure ornaments of a Portuguese Lady, who never economises her ornaments, but always empties the sum total of her trinkets upon her, and were they ten times as many would continue to stick them somewhere or other about her person rather than suffer them to stay at home when their Mistress is abroad. They are always in their Sunday clothes. Whenever they appear in publick like a Snail they carry all they are worth upon their backs. In general they are not pretty. Their complexions are too sallow. But I have seen one or two of the higher class who really had very considerable pretensions to beauty. They are indolent because they have really nothing to employ them. They are ignorant because they have never been taught that it was necessary to know any thing and they soon see they know as much as their Mothers. To shew you that the inordinate Love of finery affects the low as well as the high I cannot forbear mentioning that the woman who we employed as Washerwoman, a little short, thickset, fat, snubby nosed creature, of a true Nankeen colour came on board with a gold brazil charm round her Neck and a large Topaz cross hanging from it, a Topaz ring on her finger, Fine earrings and a lace Cloak, though living in a house which stank enough to poison a pole cat. So much for the Ladies.

The lower order of Men are in proportion as fond of dress, as indolent, and as ostentatious. All their Finery is on the outside. They will make great sacrifices for shew – But in their houses they are mean, dirty, and miserable. The Shopkeepers are exceedingly wanting in civility and do not appear to me to care in the least for your custom not always condescending to answer you themselves, but referring you to their Slaves.

The Common People are notoriously revengeful, and when they quarrel generally stab the object of their anger. Few nights pass without being marked by the assassination of some poor English man, who, I believe generally provokes the quarrel, by his drunkenness or by his intrigues.

Of the Slaves here, I believe I have before mentioned that there are in the city at least 30,000. There is a regular Slave Market in the town. They are in general very stout, athletic, laborious set of people and do all kinds of work, being employed not only as domestic Servants but to dig, to build, to fish, in short do anything. Sometimes one is shocked at seeing Gangs of ten or twelve slaves chained together by day by the neck, and dragging after them sledges, very heavily laden with cotton or coffee or other materials and making the most horrible noises. Those, however, are the slaves who have attempted to run away or have committed some other heinous offence. In general they are tolerably well treated – when a Portuguese of the lower order scrapes enough money together to buy a

Slave, he just gives him something to cover his nakedness, then sending him adrift for the day, tells him that he expects him to return in the evening with a dollar, or if he fails, he must expect a flogging. The poor devil then goes to the market and employs himself in carrying the articles that purchasers, buy; and should he not get enough that way, steals the rest, which he prefers to a flogging. No slave is allowed to wear shoes, till he has obtained his freedom, and when that happens they are immediately enlisted and sent to the mines. But I must now proceed to the Royal Family.

The Queen of Portugal is a poor, mad creature, and I believe never makes her appearance in publick. The Royal Authority being exercised by her son the Prince of the Brazils, under the title of Prince Regent . His Wife the Princess of the Brazils, a Princess of the unfortunate House of Spain, is by no means a pleasant looking woman and sometime ago, was not supposed to be on very good terms with her husband. But I believe they are now reconciled. Her great Favourite was Sir Sydney Smith (who was much admired by the Ladies here) who advised to assume the Government of the Spanish dominions in South America as Regent, which was supposed to have been the cause of the coolness between him and the Prince who sided with Lord Strangford and opposed the Plan. Their family is a very fine one: the eldest Daughter being a remarkably fine Girl of the age of 18, and one of the younger is still more beautiful. The Sons are not so handsome as the daughters. The youngest Brother of Ferdinand the 7th of Spain is at present residing at this Court, and is supposed to wish to marry one of his cousins, but he is a stupid vulgar Lout and they have all refused him. He is also as ugly as a Baboon, the Prince Regent whom I have often seen, is a lusty fat and heavy looking man; and does not appear to have any Majesty or Dignity about him. He is not tall but thick and clumsy in his figure, has a sallow complexion and an unassuming countenance, and is altogether plain and unprepossessing in his appearance. He may be said to live in public for he is constantly standing at the Balcony of his palace shewing himself to everybody. On his appearance there all the officers below take off their Hats; and he himself bows to such foreigners as may happen to be passing. At about 3 o'clock he usually goes in his carriage to a Palace he has about 4 Miles from the Town and is followed by the Princess and Family in their carriage which is a plain English Coach and I believe the only in the country; they are always accompanied by their Confessor and escorted by a Party of Dragoons. The Prince is supposed to be very discontented and anxious to return to his European Dominions about which he indulges in the most sanguine expectations and he has been heard to express extreme dislike of this country, which in proper hands and under an attentive Government might be made one of the richest on Earth, in every production. On his first arrival here, he was very popular but he soon lost the affections of his new Subjects. This is partly owing to the abominable Government he brought over with him. For there is no doubt the Brazilians enjoyed greater liberty, and commerce was more encouraged under the Viceroy than under the Prince and [it is] partly owing to the unpopularity of three brothers of the name of Labatos, Men of low origin who are his favourites, who manage everything and who without the name possess more than the power of his Ministers. Upon these Men, though undeserving of the smallest confidence, though haughty, domineering and insolent as they are low, he lavishes all his favours, and submits himself generally to their guidance. To convince you that it is impossible either for the Government or the administration of it to be otherwise than unpopular, I will now proceed to say something concerning it. It is in the present exercise of it completely despotick. There is no Liberty nor is there any security for either person or property. Since the arrival of the Prince a complete check has been given to commerce, and all encouragement withheld from Agriculture or Industry of any kind and a Soil, with which a little care and cultivation might be made to produce anything that Nature produces in the greatest perfection is now utterly neglected. Property is more particularly insecure. When the Prince sees or his Favourites direct his attention to any place or house belonging to any of his Subjects that pleases him or them, he immediately sends his orders to the possessor to give it up to whoever the Prince shall appoint and at a moments notice. This the poor man is obliged to do, and the only compensation he receives is the amount of a valuation made by the <u>Prince's Agent alone</u>, there is no appeal. In this manner on his arrival were the Brazilians of Rank deprived of their houses and Estates which had been transmitted to them from their Ancestors, to make room for the more favoured strangers who accompanied their Prince.

One man, indeed, backed by his rank and popularity saved his house by his Spirit. This was the Conde d'Amos, late Viceroy of the Brazils a

Man of the first Character, information and honour of any of the Prince's Subjects. On the arrival of the Prince having made great preparations for his reception as the shortness of time would permit, he gave up the Viceregal Palace and his authority and retired to his Country Seat, the beauty of which attracted the attention of the Labatos. Upon their suggestions, the Prince who is supposed to have been discontented with the preparations made for him by the Court, gave it to one of the brothers, who was sent to the Count to demand him to give up his house, and Labatos added that as he had no convenient residence, he should expect the Count to have it ready for his reception on the following day. Indignant at this insolence the Count told him that if he did not immediately retire he should kick him downstairs. This was of course conveyed to the ears of the Prince, who banished the Count. The poor man found the means to obtain an interview with the Princess and represented to her the hardship of this treatment, and his readiness to comply with all the proper commands of his Prince and by her interference the Banishment was revoked, but the Count was not allowed to come to Court. The Affair soon began to be talked of and the Prince did not choose to press his demand any further so that the Count preserved both his Honour and his House.

Much Formality I am told prevails at the Court of Rio Janeiro on the regular Court days. But the Prince allows Strangers to be introduced to him in a private way in the Evening and thus dispenses with the formality of a Court Dress. This is unfortunate. I did not know in time enough, and this Ignorance was the cause of my not choosing to be presented. When the time was past, Lord Strangeford acquainted me with the Circumstance. The Governor and Lieutenant Governor both went in full dress; were received very politely and the Prince entered a good deal into conversation (in French) with the Lieutenant Governor who was educated in France and was once in the French Service. The Prince having ordered them a box at the Opera they went there after Court and said they were much entertained. My not having been there made me forget to say anything of this amusement, which is almost the only one in St Sebastians. I will therefore proceed to it now.

I am informed that the Opera House is about the size of Haymarket Theatre and that it is very neat and much frequented by the Prince. The Boxes are all private and the admission to the Pit is 6 English shillings. The Singing is very good indeed, excellent and the acting is also very good. The two nights are Tuesdays and <u>Sundays</u> of which the latter is the principal. The Performance begins at Eight or a little after and the lateness of the Hour with the necessity of returning on Board at night, was the cause of my not having been there which I rather lament, as I should have been able to give you a more animated and complete Picture of it.

The Nobility here are in general very poor: more especially those who accompanied their Prince, as they were obliged to leave their possessions in Portugal. Among these are the Marquis de Pombal, who was the richest Subject in Portugal, has now been deprived of all his wealth and splendour and is now reduced to live in St Sebastian on the niggardly bounty of the Prince. They are in general very proud and ignorant and though they are poor they are very fond of expensive decorations and rather splendid shows particularly on their Wedding and Feast Days. All their Money is spent in purposes of ostentation not comfort.

Of the Priests, who are very important class of Men here, these are great numbers; they are treated with great respect, and veneration, have yet considerable Influence, and are certainly a very decent, civil set of people, and the best informed persons in the nation. To Strangers, they are remarkably polite, and attentive, and I never passed one, without his pulling off his hat to me. But though the Portuguese are still very superstitious, they are not so priest ridden as they once were; and recent events have very much curtailed their Revenue and the Power of the Clergy. But the forms of the Religion are still as regularly kept up and as splendidly solemnized as formerly. The same Expense and show are displayed on the festival for a favourite Saint, the same regard and attention are paid to Lent and Fast days and Saint days. The Keeping of these last is certainly a great hindrance to all public business and a great delay to all commercial affairs: For all publick offices are shut up and though the shops continue open, the Owners of them are more careless than usual about shewing their goods and shew still less than their ordinary attention to their customers. The Feast of the Assumption is kept here very devoutly and took place during our stay. The Eve of it was ushered in by discharge of Cannons, processions of Nuns, Friars and the Host, and a great display of fireworks. The following morning the Prince Regent and all his family were present at the celebration of Grand Mass in his own chapel.

... The Organ Service afterwards was very grand and impressive and the singing very beautiful. Besides the Royal Family a great number of the nobility were there, very gorgeously arrayed, and among them were some very beautiful women.

… The carriages in St Sebastian's are very small, and have a curious appearance to Strangers. They are a species of Cabriolet or Caloush, solid on all sides having no doors and having the Front closed with loose Leather, which opens or shuts as the owner pleases. The wheels, which in general are only two, are very high; and the body so small as to allow room for only two indeed Three persons in a carriage would almost certainly raise a mob. They are drawn by two Mules, one of which carries the Driver, who is often a Negro. It is in fact the true Gil Blas Carriage such is represented in the Pictures in the old editions of that book. The palanquins are very splendid, differing from those seen before in containing a handsome chair which is certainly I should think more comfortable then those used at Madeira in which the rider is obliged to recline. These Palanquins are generally entirely closed with handsome Curtains when they contain Ladies.

The Canoes used upon the Harbour in which the country people bring their fruits and vegetables to Market from the county opposite St Sebastian's are very singular. Many of them are of great length and breadth, and consist of the solid Trunk of a Tree scooped out; they are paddled along by Negroes with wooden paddles, who frequently make use of a large square Mat, by way of a Main Sail. The after part of many of these Canoes, is covered over, and serves as the House of the owner of the Canoe. They appear to be remarkably dangerous but it is astonishing how they load them and with what skill they navigate them. I shall now proceed to say something of the country around St Sebastian and its production with which I shall close this imperfect sketch.

… The Mountains are remarkably fantastic in their forms and most of them are covered with Groves of the most beautiful Mangoes, and Orange Trees. The Country abounds with Cotton Coffee, Cocoa, Rice, Tobacco and Sugar. These are all remarkably cheap and good, Oranges both sweet and bitter grow quite wild, and are hardly of any value.

I have never seen an original Native of this Country. They do not often come to the City: though during the time I was there, A Brazilian Indian was in the Town; but I was never lucky enough to find him out. These Indians make beautiful hats, baskets and other Things of the bark of some Tree, which they cover very tastefully and bring to St Sebastians to sell: but when they have once got into the Portuguese shops, they are very dear, especially as the colour quickly fades and they are soon worn out.

Fowls are remarkably fine and sell for about 4d each, which is by no means cheap, this however is the market price. The Turkies and Ducks are very large indeed and bear a proportionate price. As to the Meat, the beef is very coarse and poor; but such as it is sells very cheap indeed not more than 2d per lb ... The mutton is much better but it is scarce and therefore dearer; about 9d per lb. Pork is very good, and Wild Hops are plentiful. I never heard of Veal here and of the milch cows Sir James Gambier told me, that whenever the calves were taken away from them they immediately ceased to give milk, and on that account, he was obliged to give up one third to the Calves and the Remainder himself.

The horses of Rio Janeiro are small indeed, but are very active and safe and pleasant to ride. A very good one may be procured for £10 or £12. A greater value is set on the Mules, though in my opinion they are not as pleasant. They are very obstinate, kick most terribly sometimes and require the most regular exercise. But on the other hand they are very beautiful, handy and surefooted, do a great deal of work and by their slowness suit the Gravity of their Masters. A good Mule sells here at a great price.

The Vegetables are remarkably fine especially the cabbage, lettuce and yam, the latter when well boiled is dry, mealy, clean and white in colour and in short an excellent substitute for Potatoes. In its outward appearance it is like a log of Wood, and it will keep for ever, the Sweet Potato is very disagreeable to me.

... The Brazilian Gold is very pure, fine and delicate in colour. It sells for £3.12 the ounce. The silver is not reckoned so good as the English. The only taste the Portuguese display is in the making of these Gold Chains. In the ornaments they make of their precious Stones and the setting of them they are very gaudy, clumsy and deficient in either elegance or taste. Silver here is 4s 6d an ounce. Of precious Stones the principal are the Topazes, Amethysts and Diamonds. The Brazilian Topaz is the most beautiful in the world, it is hard, clear, and of a bright yellow.

The Brazilian diamonds were at one time supposed to be inferior to those of the East. But Jewellers now set an equal value upon them. His death or banishment to the mines for any Subject but those employed in the Mines to be seen with a rough Diamond in their possession [means] that all the diamonds are in Foreign Countries. The Produce of the diamond Mines belongs exclusively to the Crown and a vast quantity were lately sent to our Government in the *Diana* Frigate as security for the repayment of money lent. The Diamond mines are situated about 600 miles inland; and the Portuguese Government is so jealous that no person, found there without a license is allowed to return, but condemned to work there for life. At present, therefore, they are little known but much reliable information concerning them is soon likely to be circulated, as the Prince has lately granted permission to an English Scientific Jeweller connected with Rundle and Bridge to visit them... The Prince is supposed to have the finest collection of precious Stones in the World. He succeeded in bringing them from Portugal and they are of immense value...What a Prize Buonaparte missed!

The Ounce and the Serpent are the most formidable animals in Brazil. The latter are of an immense size and very numerous. But I never saw any. But a little animal which I'm sorry to say is as common in New South Wales does more mischief than either, not to the person, but to all wearing apparel. This is the White Ant which will eat in one night through Wood of great thickness, and against which nothing will avail but incessant vigilance. Lady Gambier told me that it eat into all their trunks, and that she had lost £200 worth of Things. They make their attacks in Myriads.

Officer's mess room on board a ship of war, c1820

Speaking a vessel off the Cape of Good Hope, Augustus Earle, 1824

VUE DE LA SALLE DE SPECTACLE SUR LA PLACE *DO ROCIO*, À RIO DE JANEIRO.

Vue de la salle de spectacle sur la place Do Rocio, Rio de Janeiro, Paris, 1822

New South Wales, view of Sydney from the east side of the cove, John Heaviside Clark, June 1810

10

Letters from Rio

To Father Rio August 18 1809

…Mr Harris in company with Mr Johnston, Mr Macarthur (who have already sailed from Rio for England) a Mr Jamison and another gentleman had arrived at this Port from N.S Wales in a Vessel called the Admiral Gambier about 7 weeks ago after a passage of 11 weeks around Cape Horn. As they called on board the Dromedary, to pay their respects to the New Governor, I did not miss the opportunity of sharing some conversation with them … Mr Harris gave me some information respecting myself and the colony of NSW which I'm sure will gratify you and my dearest mother as much as it did me. Mr Harris who has been a long time in NS Wales is the Surgeon to the NS Wales Corps, now the 102nd Regiment and Mr Jamison who is Surgeon General to the Colony both gave a most favourable account of it in every respect. They both describe my house as being pleasant one and having an excellent situation and having an excellent Garden. They say they left the colony in great plenty … I and the Members of my Family are entitled to our regular Rations that is 7lb of beef, 4 1/2 lb of Pork 7lb of Bread and a proportion of Butter, Rice and Sugar every week which at any rate will be sufficient to maintain the Servants. My fees too I am told will amount to at least £800 …

In the Colony, however, there is very Little Specie and excepting some few dollars of the Copper Currency. The only circulating medium is promissory Notes issued by different individuals and which generally return to them in about three months. But Barter is a very common and always very profitable mode of purchasing goods.

Through George Knox's means I got at Madeira a letter to Sir James Gambier the Consul General here and from Mrs Knox a letter to her cousin here Mr Staples. On my arrival I found the latter had gone to Rio Plata – but his partner Mr MacNeil, a genteel young man, extremely civil... was kind enough to offer us a cottage he has about three miles from the town, but we declined because I thought the distance too great and because we were very comfortable on board..

Sir James Gambier has also been very civil to us – but as his House out of Town and is filled by his Family, which is large, he apologised for not being able to offer us a Bed. Sir James is a very pleasant and hospitable Man and lives in great stile here, superior indeed to that of the Prince Regent. Lady Gambier is a very charming woman, pleasant, affable, handsome and hospitable. Their Family consists of two fine Boys and 3 girls. A Miss Snell, her sister, also lives with them and is very accomplished and pleasant. We dined there on Friday last. The Governor and Mrs Macquarie were of the Party ... his house is in the Indian stile, very pretty.. Everything was served on Plate and the Entertainment was equal to that of the first nobleman in England.

Lord Strangeford is generally disliked here – he lives in no Kind of stile, is very inhospitable, and is very ceremonious, indeed a complete Courtier.

... One thing for which I am at a loss is how to direct my enclosure to Mr Cooke. If to you at Moulsey, I am fearful of postage to my Brother as he has no Clerk his Doors might be shut I would therefore advise him to call at the Office – tho' I think I shall request Mr Cooke to direct the Packet to you.

To Mother August 17 1809

I trust you will find my Journal down to my arrival at St Sebastians, my account of Madeira and that of Porto Praya. They all are written in a hasty manner for I do not find the Confusion of a Ship and the little little inconveniences which must be submitted to there calculated to serious or continued attention. My account of Madeira must be considered only as a Sketch of the impression made on my mind by a pleasant Island after a tedious and unpleasant Voyage, and even if it should be exaggerated is at least a true transcript of my feelings.

[My son] is particularly fond of a Black Hindoo Servant of Colonel Macquarie's and frequently cries to go to him …

Colonel Macquarie … has already requested me to accept the place of Judge of the Admiralty Court there, in short my prospects there are flattering – Elizabeth is I think likely to make a valuable servant very clean and well behaved.

George turns out very well – he has the usual fault of Boys – thoughtlessness, but he is very willing, sober and clean and careful of his clothes. He waits every week at table and writes a very good hand. In every respect I have reason to feel comfortable and to entertain the most Sanguine hopes of the future.

We generally have a little luncheon in the Middle of the day but we cannot always have cold meat, for what is not used at dinner is either eaten by the servants or given to the poor soldiers or their wives who may be sick. Our dinners are very good in point of eating and drinking for we always have plenty of fresh meat.

… The worst part of our dinner is the slovenly mode of serving it up. They put as many dishes on the table at a time as to make the table very uncomfortable. In short there is no stile about it or neatness.

We take a frugal supper bread and cheese and wine and Water. We usually have a rubber of whist, or at Mrs Macquarie's request I read a play, a farce aloud in her Cabin and we retire at ten o'clock. This is the uniform time of our lives except that the Ship is a prison we ought to feel ourselves very comfortable.

I am afraid you will think me diffuse on telling you at such length what we eat and what we drink! But you do not know how grateful the sight of fresh fish, fresh fruit and fresh vegetables is to those who have been many weeks deprived of them.

The Ball at Sir James Gambier's was very elegant. The Rooms are large and lofty and very elegantly furnished. At the front of the house is a spacious Verandah which was very well lighted up and made an excellent Promenade. We sat down about 60 to a very admirable supper, served on Silver and beautiful China and did not reach our ship till past four o'clock in the morning.

Invited to a ball or supper by Captain Yeo of the Confiance, I am told the Quarter Deck was splendidly illuminated but it rained and blew very hard that none of us were able to go...

Rio is in a swamp, unwholesome vapours are very prejudicial to those who live here.

Letter to Jeffery Bent August 20 1809

...If it had not been for the Hindostan we should have made a very fine passage. When the Hindostan has every sail set we can only carry our Topsails and these were lowered. Indeed She is in no respect calculated for the long Voyage for which she is destined. She is an old crank Ship, badly caulked, badly favoured and by her bad sailing increases the Risk of the Voyage. How My Lord Mulgrave appointed such a Vessel is astonishing. All the punishment I wish him is that he should be condemned to sail round the world in her himself.

[Of Rio] Colonel Macquarie who has been in almost every port in the world was quite in raptures and says he never saw anything equal to it. It is very dirty, the streets are narrow.

My spirits, thank God, are pretty good though I now and then have some severe fits of dejection when I indulge in thoughts of my family, my friends and also England ...

I am the first by most extraordinary coincidence to communicate the loss of the Port au Prince[1]. She was taken by the Savages at one of the Feejee Islands who slaughtered the improvident Captain and his Crew which were nearly all destroyed by the ravages of Scurvy.

[Of Jamison and Macarthur travelling to England] very fortunately for them and us, for Colonel Macquarie had positive orders to send Colonel Johnston home under arrest and I should have had to try Mr Macarthur.

[Of Mr Harris] You will no doubt see him, he will give you further account of the place than I am able to do, and will shew you drawings of the Town and some private Country Houses in particular of his which is very beautiful. He has 130 head of deer there.

There are many necessarys which when I arrive at Sydney I may find at an extravagant price. Most of these necessaries are to be procured here at the cheapest rate. I have therefore determined to buy a stock of these for my consumption.

It would be hard to be obliged to give 1s 6d or two shillings per pound for worse sugar in Sydney than can get here for two pence per pound. Washing here is also singularly expensive and very bad as much as 9d a shirt and the rest in proportion.

For the remainder of the dollars that I got at Madeira and for which I got 5s 6d I get only 4s 6d each which is the current price of dollars and this alone is a considerable loss to me..

Endnote

1   *The Port au Prince was Robert Bent's Man o'War which he had instructed to go privateering in 1808 and, failing that to go whaling in the South Seas. There was one survivor of the capture of the ship, John Mariner, and his story of privateering and life in Tonga was published in 1820. J. Martin, An Account of the Natives of the Tonga Islands of the South Pacific, Charles Ewer,Boston, 1820.*

11

Journal from Rio to the Cape

Thursday August 24th

The Wind being yesterday very favourable for us, soon took us out of the Harbour of Rio, and has since continued to blow pretty fresh from the north east. In consequence of Mrs Jones, Mrs Macquarie's Servant having left her, to set up as a Milliner at Rio, an arrangement has been made respecting the Cabins very convenient to us ... I got some Marmalade at Rio, and laid on a good number of Eggs, which I preserved in the following manner; Having broke an Egg or two I separated the Yolk from the White then I rubbed the remainder of the Eggs over with the White and let them dry; I then rubbed them over again; and when the White was quite dry on the Shell I put them into small Barrells or Kegs, and covered them with plenty of Bran.

Friday August 25th

The Wind still continues to blow fresh from the same quarter. At Noon we were in Lat. 26 46' S and the Longl. 42 07 W Having ran 120 miles in the last 24 Hours and we have great hopes of reaching the Cape in a Month though we have 3600 Miles to run. I am afraid the water is not very good for something or other affects my Bowels. The Colonel and Captain have already had a similar complaint, and attribute it to the same cause. Yet I never drink it unmixed with Wine. In the evening I was very unwell and very feverish. I went to bed early, But did not sleep till morning.

Sunday August 27th

I feel quite recovered and strong again this morning but I must confess that I was not sorry that the freshness of the Breeze and the swell of the Sea prevented us from having divine Service. At Noon we were in Latitude 30 21' South and Long 38 20 W and had run 150 miles. But though I did not read Prayers this morning I was not idle in my clerical Department For I married a Soldier's widow, whose husband I had buried only 2 months before, to a very decent Sailor, in the presence of the Colonel, Captain etc. In the evening the wind freshened very much.

Monday August 28th

A great deal of rain fell during the night. Of all weather, I think wet weather the most unpleasant on board Ship. The Damp reaches everything, and it is hardly possible to avoid catching cold. The Rains lasted all day with great violence, and almost blew a Gale, and the motion of the Ship was very great. We were quite uncomfortable ... At Noon we were in Lat 39 35' S and Long 35 29' W. – and had ran 164 miles.

Tuesday August 29th

In the morning it was nearly a dead calm and our progress had of course been little. A Boat came from the *Hindostan* by which we were all glad to hear that their Sick had decreased in number and were all convalescent. The Swell is still considerable.

Wednesday August 30th

This day was very fine, and there was a tolerable Breeze, but the Swell so great as to render writing almost impossible ... At noon we were in Latitude 32 25' S and Long: 33 5' W.

Thursday August 31st

A fine fresh Breeze at S.W with a heavy swell, which being right aft, makes us roll terribly. No writing. At Noon in Lat 33 01 S and Long 33 5 W.

Friday September 1st

... The Breeze having continued all the Night, we had made 169 miles in the last 24 hours and were at noon in Lat 33 32' S and Long. 27 52' W at 1 pm while we were going at the rate of 10 knots an hour, in a very heavy Sea, one of the Carpenters, a very fine Young Man who was employed in mending the Scuttles, fell overboard, and the Ship was instantly brought to and the Jolly Boat lowered and manned almost immediately, The Poor Fellow could not be saved, He was a great loss. This accident damped all our Spirits.

Saturday September 2nd

We had a very unpleasant night, as the Ship rolled Gunnel under, every time. In the middle of the Night, my Wash hand stand broke from its lashings and chair, Table, Basin etc., made a hideous uproar. The cot touched the ceiling every roll, All was confusion. At Break of day I rose and got the Carpenter to lash up my stand again, which fortunately was not broken. At Noon we had run 182 miles and were in Lat 33 34' S and Long 24 18' W. Towards evening the Breeze fell away and we amused ourselves at whist. The Colonel and myself are generally partners and mostly lose, but we never exceed Silver Threepences.

Sunday September 3rd

The morning was quite calm and beautifully fine and the day was a Day of Adventures. At 8 o'clock am the Captain hooked a large Shark, but hauling it up it broke the line and went away with the Hook in its Jaws. A great number of Birds were about the ship and among them several Albatrosses.

Captain Cleaveland of the 73rd shot three of those Birds which we had improperly called Pintado Birds. They were very handsome blacklegged and web footed. At 11am read Prayers in Publick. At Noon our Lat 33 36' and Long 23 4' W and the distance run 61 miles. At one o'clock we saw several Whales playing and spouting at no great distance from the Ship. They were not very large; though they spouted water at least 20 feet high. At 2pm another Shark took the Hook and afforded us much diversion. The Glistening of his purple Skin, his exertions, strength and activity were amazing. But whilst he was playing and striking the Water with his Tail and when we had just heard that there was a still larger shark about the Bows of the ship, Mr Sullivan Signal Officer leaning over the Poop from his overeagerness to see the sport, fell overboard, close to the Shark, which very luckily was then hooked, though not fast. As it was quite calm, he was taken up without sustaining any damage, but a good ducking. Immediately, the Shark also escaped, the Remaining Shark then determined to try his luck. He came swimming about the Hook and at length I saw him turn on his Back and swallow the Bait, a piece of Salt Pork very greedily. After playing him for some time a Sailor was sent down who let a running bowling knot over his Shoulders, by which he was soon drawn up and lowered on the Quarter Deck. He was a Blue Shark, about 2 years old, and measured nine feet in length from the Tip of his head to that of his Tail. In the evening I read to Colonel and Mrs M. The Captain and Eliza, one of the Bishop of London's Lectures.

Monday September 4th

A fine fresh Breeze, sprung up at last night, and this morning we were swimming at the rate of 6 Knots an hour. As we approached the Cape we got up a new set of sails, having completely worn out one set, since we left England. At Noon we were in Lat. 34 14' S and Long. 21 43' W, distance run 78 miles. We are now south of Table Bay; but as our own Commodore still persists in steering one Point South of East, we imagine he wishes to make the Island of Tristan da Cunha, a high, barren uninhabited Island visible at

25 Leagues distance in Lat 36 27' S and Long. 13 17' W. We are all sorry for this as it takes us two degrees south of the Cape and exposes us to violent Gales. The Thermometer at 60°.

Tuesday, September 5th

A strong steady breeze, but a raw, thick, unpleasant day. My little Boy is quite stout and fat. We have had a fine run of 175 miles in the last 24 hours and are now in latitude 35 37' S and in Long. 18 26' W, being considerably South of the Cape and 298 miles from Tristan de Cunha. Our Commodore has hauled his Wind, but it will still not now permit us to steer East. At 2pm A fresh breeze and ship running nine knots an hour. Mr Carter, Surgeon of the 73rd and his Wife dined with us, today, and in the evening we played a Rubber, Mrs C was my partner, she plays even worse than her husband.

Wednesday September 6th

We have just been a fortnight from Rio and have hitherto had a most favourable Voyage. This day our Run has been better than any since we left England. Having gone 193 miles. At noon we were in Lat: 35 49' S and in Long. 15 26' W. Tristan de Cunha bearing S 65 E at a distance of 115 miles. We are now fast returning into the Longitude of Greenwich when our Hours will be the same. At present there is more than an Hour difference; four Minutes are allowed for each degree of Longitude, when to the Westward we are later in that proportion and when to the Eastward earlier. The Colonel has bet a Rupee with me that we shall anchor in Table Bay next Monday week.

Thursday September 7th

This morning the Commodore made the Signal for us to make all sail to the south south east for land. The Deuce take this Island Hunting! The day was excessively hazy and wet. At Noon we were in Lat: 36 15' S and in Long. 11 41 W having ran by observation 184 miles. Tho' by our Log we had run 208 miles. Tristan de Cunha at this time bore South, distant 69 miles according to the Admiralty charts which lay it down in Lat. 37 15' S and in Long 11 40' W.

Friday September 8th

The Morning was very wet and cold and at Noon the thermometer was as low as 57. What variety of Climate have I already experienced. At Noon we were in Lat. 36 10' S and Long. 8 5' W, distance ran 123 miles and Tristan da Cunha bearing S 60 W distance 149 miles. Though I do not mention my Morning's employment. They are not by any means spent idly by either Eliza or myself. It takes some time drawing up and copying my Journal, and my letters of the different places I visit. For I always copy each to be able to supply deficiencies if my parcels should miscarry. Besides this work I read a good deal, and lest I should lose any of my Law which God knows I can little spare I read some every day. When I am tired Eliza in her turn reads to me. When she is working I frequently read to her. The Evenings I hardly call my own; as it would be too unsocial to shut oneself in one's Cabin; and refuse to make up a whist party.

Saturday September 9th

In the course of last night we had a dead calm and a very heavy rain with a heavy Swell and violent rolling. This morning was very wet than which nothing can be more unpleasant on board Ship. Every Cabin is damp and everybody is uncomfortable. At Noon we were in Lat 35 45 S and in Long 6 26 W. Distance run 84 miles, The Cape of Good Hope bearing N 86 E 1186 miles. Thermometer 60.

Sunday September 10th

A most delightful clear day and a strong dry wind animated us all. It comes doubly welcome after the late damp weather. It was no Day of Rest with me for I read prayers in publick by which I caught cold, and afterwards churched a Woman, and christened her Child. His name was Edward Bradshaw. At Noon we were in Lat 35 32 S and in Long: 2 47' W having run 182 miles and the Cape bearing N 87 E so 29 miles distant, it is a great amusement to have our daily progress marked on the Admiralty Chart and no-one who has not been in a similar situation can conceive the pleasure we feel, when it is great, and our extreme anxiety at 12 o' clock when the Observation is taken.

Monday September 11th

The Wind continues to hold, but the day is not quite so clear, and promising. At noon we were in Lat. 32. 22 S in Lon 66 58 E – distance run 194 miles. The Cape bearing N 88 E distant 850 miles could we but continue this rate of going!

Tuesday September 12th

The Wind continued very moderate during the night, but most unfortunately for us at 10 AM it became quite foul, blowing hard at S.E. At 11am the Commodore spoke us and we were all glad to hear that his Sick list was reduced to one person. At noon we were in Latitude 34 36' S and Long 2 37' E. The distance ran 86 miles and the Cape bearing N 89 E. distant 784 miles. We this day saw a great number of large Birds and Albatrosses of great size. Several were shot; but as no boats were lowered, we could not get them.

Wednesday September 18th

In the night we had very much pitching, and at AM Wind blowing very fresh in our teeth. At Noon we were in Lat 35 52'. Long 2 43 E. Distance run 67 Miles, all out of our way.

Thursday September 14th

Wind still directly at East, but more moderate. At noon in Lat. 37 5' S Long. 2 56' E – distance run South 74 miles; the Cape bearing N 79 E distance 773 miles. Thermometer at 57 Thank God! My little boy is as hearty as possible and the Officer's cow gives plenty of milk.

Friday September 15th

The wind blew fresh during the night, but again moderated this morning. At Noon we were in Lat 33 24 and in Long. 3 45' 30 E the Cape bearing N 72 E distant 774 miles. For some days past it has been very cold, but this day the Thermometer was as low as 56 At 6pm the Breeze altered two points in our favour and we now hauled up to the east south east. Played our usual rubber and went to Bed in better spirits Though I have a bad cold and also a Sore Throat.

Saturday September 16th

This morning there are great hopes of a change, and at 10am we were able to lay east by south. At 11 the Commodore made the Signal to lay E by N which the changes of Wind now enabled us to do. At Noon we were in Lat. 39 2' S and Long 5 22' 30 E. The Cape bearing S 62 E 637 Miles distant having ran 184 miles.

Sunday September 17th

We are all animated by a beautiful clear and dry day and strong favourable Breeze. At Noon we were in Lat 27 55' S and in Long 7 48' 30" E . Distance runs 133 miles and the Cape bearing N 66 E distant 504 miles. At 1pm I baptised the Captain's Stewards' Infant by the name of Sarah Henderson. I forgot to mention that yesterday I buried a poor little Infant whom I had christened about three weeks before. There was an immense number of very large Albatrosses and the birds flying about the Ship, the whole day, and among them several Cape Hens which are entirely black but none were shot. The Day was very cold, the Thermometer being as low as 50.

Monday September 18th

During the Night there was little Wind and the Noise of the straining of the Poop, the Creaking of the Bulkhead and the screeching of the Spanker Boom from the heavy rolling was as great, as to deprive me, whom a severe cold rendered uneasy, of all Rest. The Morning was almost as calm and much warmer than yesterday, but the Swell was long and high. A Boat was sent on board the *Hindostan* and brought us the news that, the ship was now quite healthy…A Child had his hand jammed to pieces in the rolling by the falling of the Carpenter's Bench.

Tuesday September 19th

I am sorry to say we have again a foul wind blowing fresh at S.E and God knows when we shall get into Port. A few days ago, I opened a packing case, containing a Tin box with Eliza's dresses and found them all safe. At Noon we were in Latitude 36. 07 S and Longitude 11 18 E, distance run 86 miles and the Cape N 72 E distance 366 miles. My sore throat has gone and my cold is much better.

Wednesday September 20th

The pitching of the Vessel was so violent during the night that we had very little Sleep. In the Morning the wind was still contrary and there was an immense Swell, but the Breeze was decreasing. At noon we were in Lat: 34, 40' S and Long: 11 43. The distance was 90 miles. The bearings at the Cape were N 88.2 E distance 334 miles.

Thursday September 21st

This Morning there was but very little Wind, I amused myself in reading to Eliza, Miss Hamilton's excellent novel of *The Modern Philosophers*. My cold is not quite so well as it was yesterday. At Noon we found ourselves in Lat. 34 32' S and Long 13 3' E, the distance run in the last 24 hours was 65 miles and the Cape of Good Hope fore N. 89 E about 265 miles, and as we now have a fine five Knot breeze we have hopes of anchoring there on Saturday.

Friday September 22nd

At Eight am there was a noble Breeze and the Ship was going through the water at the rate of 8 knots an hour. At 11 am by order of the Commodore made sail to make the land, for by his calculation he is 67 miles nearer the Land than we are by ours. At Noon we were in Lat. 33 S and Long. 15 53'. The Distance ran was 140 Miles and the Cape bore N 83 E distant 122 Miles. We had a very fine breeze at NNW and were all day occupied in the pleasing Labour of preparing to go on shore. My cold too was much better. After making all sail without seeing Land for seven hours which proved the accuracy of our observations. At Six PM we were recalled. In the Morning we saw a strange Sail which in the afternoon the Commodore came up with, and spake. At 7.30pm the Commodore bore down to hail us and when very close to us, the Tiller Rope of the *Hindostan* gave way, and her head instantly swung round to the Wind. We were all alarmed, and had not our ship answered her Helm very readily we should have been foul of each other. Having repaired the Damage Captain Pascoe spoke us and told us that the strange vessel was a Brig from London in three months, which confirmed the good news we had at Rio relative to the defeat of Napoleon by the Arch Duke Charles. I could not help hoping that she contained Letters for me from my friends.

Saturday September 23rd

We lay to from 12 till 4am for fear of getting near a very low and dangerous Island at the Entrance of Table Bay, called Robber or Penguin Island. At 4am made all sail, the Wind being right aft. At 6am the Morning was very thick and Hazy. At 7.30 it cleared up and the Bold termination of the Continent of Africa was distinctively seen. At nine Table Land which is very high and massive, was in full view at about E distant 18 miles. The Breeze was very fresh and there was a strong following Sea, which made the Ship roll excessively. The guns on each side were alternately under every Roll. On this passage I have two observations to make, one of which is that no one hardly ever made the Cape which is proverbially tempestuous, with so calm a sea and in such fine weather. The other is that during the whole passage from America to Africa, a distance of 4000 miles, not a Single Day passed without our seeing Flocks of Birds, all indeed of the aquatic kind of various Species – this surely proves that either there must be many more Islands scattered over this part of the south Atlantic; or that the approach of Birds is not by any means a certain Indication of the Vicinity of Lands. The day was now uncommonly fine; About 11am we closed in with the Land and about ¼ before 12 at Noon we anchored in Table Bay, immediately opposite Cape Town and about Two Miles from the shore. We made land at the exact time the Observations of the Captain gave us reason to expect, which is ample and highly satisfactory proof of the accuracy of our Chronometer, and performed the Voyage from Rio to the Cape in the exact Space of one Calendar Month.

12

Letters from the Cape of Good Hope

To Mother 1 October 1809

The light Cape Wine, the only Wine that is drunk in the Dutch families has disagreed with [Eliza], which I'm told is commonly the case at first.

I think I have now got everything with me to supply a House for some time, I hope in a month's time after my arrival to be comfortable settled.

Capetown is beautiful …

The kindness of Mr G. Knox had procured me a letter from him to Mr Alexander who is Colonial Secretary and notwithstanding his connexion with Dupre I delivered it myself at the first moment I came ashore … the first words he addressed me was 'Did I not see you at Aylesbury some years ago with your father' and on my replying in the affirmative He added 'Ay Du Pre's interference in that affair cost him £20,000'. His House in the Castle is but small and not sufficient to accommodate his own family – but tho' on this account he could not invite me to live there, he walked about the whole day with me endeavouring to procure lodgings, in which I at length succeeded. Eliza has since dined there several times but I have usually been engaged to Men's parties given by the Admiral, Commander in Chief and second in command.

The lodgings tho' very comfortable are very dear. All the respectable, indeed the very first Dutch families are willing to take Strangers into their houses and provide them with lodgings, Wine and everything for a certain compensation which is certainly high … But it is now extremely difficult to prevail on any of the respectable Dutch families to receive anyone in this way – the Englishmen have so much abused and laughed at them for this custom (which in their own opinion did not lower them a jot) that they now require to be coaxed into it. There are no Dutch Inns and the English are so expensive beyond anything you can conceive. We are in the House of a Mr Brand, a Dutchman connected with the first families in this colony who is a very pleasant and sensible man. He has a very nice wife and a large young family, they live very well and do all they can to make us comfortable.

We have an excellent breakfast of coffee, fresh and charming butter, Bread, eggs, cold meat and boiled fish at half past eight. We have a very good dinner at 3, Tea at 7 and supper at half past nine, they cook, very well and their curries and rice are very good. I called on my arrival on Lord Caledon but he was not there at home. He returned my call, since that time I have been introduced as has Eliza at a subscription Ball which took place last Thursday and had a good deal of conversation. He is very young for a Governor and is very much liked here, and tho' he is distant and shy but not proud, he is remarkably attentive. This day 3rd October Eliza and myself are going to dine with him at Government House, and Mrs Alexander calls for us in his Lordship's carriage. I have already dined with the Admiral who according to report here, is not very remarkable for either the Qualities of an Admiral or a Gentleman and General Wetherall 2nd in command who is a very pleasant man and tomorrow I am to dine with General Grey, the Commander in Chief which being a Man's Party, Eliza dines with Mrs Alexander. Since we have been here I have taken several rides on Horseback and Eliza has accompanied me, as my acquaintance with the same Officers has enabled me to procure a safe horse for her. – She rides well, is by no means timid, the kind of Exercise is I think very likely to do her great good. On Thursday we mean to ride over to the celebrated Vineyard of Constantine which is about 2 hours ride from Cape Town and belongs to an Uncle of my Landlord.

Wednesday 9 October, We dined yesterday at Lord Caledon's the Party was very large, but consisted only of English people. The service of Plate was as superb as any I ever saw of the kind; Though the dinner was badly cooked in the Dutch stile which is to stew and boil everything to rags. The Dutch never roast meat and barely know what it means. The desert knives, forks and spoons were of gold. In the Evening we played at cards and about 10 sat down to a small supper. Mrs Alexander always presides at these parties which are very formal, she is rather handsome, tho' affected.

Today I am going to dine at General Grey's and Eliza was invited to Mrs Alexander's but as she had a slight sore throat, she declines exposing herself to the night air which is here very prejudicial. We intend going on board on Saturday as we are again to set sail on Sunday or Monday next …

[I have heard good accounts of the colony] Mr Alexander who is well acquainted with the situation of the Colony told me that he considered my appointment not only lucrative but conspicuous and important and likely to attract the attention of government.

He told me he himself had written to Lord Castlereagh not long ago, that he himself was willing to accept the situation of Governor of NS Wales with the same salary as is attached to his appointment here that is £3000 English currency but that the arrangements were complete. He said he certainly would not have done this if he had not conceived the settlement to be flourishing, and likely to be moreso. However he was astonished to find that my salary was so small, and conceived Ministers shabby in that respect. I wish that it was increased and that my friends could make interest for that purpose.

… You would be astonished of the dearness of every European article at the Cape, 4 shillings and a bottle of Porter 10s for Port Wine or £5 to £6 for a straw hat 7s for a pair of shoes which might be bought for 2d in England. Nothing here is cheap but wine… Mr Wilberforce Bird who is settled here has been very civil to us. Mrs Bird and I believe six daughters are with him. Eliza has been introduced we have been invited there but were engaged. If we do not go on board we are to pass next Sunday there.

He makes a good deal of money as Prize Agent, but I am told has lost by shipping. I must close this letter my dearest mother …

To Jeffery October 10 1809

I have now furnished myself with everything I shall want in NS Wales for a considerable time at a moderate expence compared with the sum they would have cost me in the Colony. Many of them I shall barter to great advantage – and except for Household Furniture which I shall procure little by little – I have little occasion for money. I have Wine, Rice, Candles, Oil, Spices, Tea, Coffee, Cocoa, Chocolate, Brandy, Gin, Flour, Salt, a Goat, Tobacco, Dried Fruits, such as Raisin, Figs etc Almonds and Honey. My Wine consists of 15 dozen of Port, a cask of Medoc Claret, containing 11 dozen which cost me £4.15. A pipe of Madeira, a pipe of Cape Wine, containing 125 gallons which cost me short of £20 and is 3 years old and some Constantia which is a present to me from Mr Alexander. Thus you see, the first two years of my housekeeping are nearly provided for. I should only wish you, when my finances will bear it to send me 15 to 20 dozen of Port in bottles and to continue it yearly. Bottles and casks are so expensive in NS Wales, that I should prefer my wine being sent in bottles and if to this a cask of sound Porter or Burton Ale, should be added I should be amply provided for, the last, however should be in the wood. One very great article of expence has been my washing.

The expensive Dearness of this article will I am sure astonish you. My bill at this place alone for this article of Expenditure is more than £10 and since I left England has cost me more than £30. At Rio they washed so badly that we were obliged to have most of our things washed over again. At Madeira they utterly spoiled me 4 dozen Napkins. Here they wash remarkably well, but the mode of washing in all these places is nearly the same. No hot water is used, the clothes are laid flat in running water and the dirt is stoned out with stones, so they frequently come home with holes in them as big as your head.

13

Letters from Sydney

Sydney Sunday March 4 1810
My Dearest Mother,

At length I have the satisfaction of informing you that we have, Thanks be to God! Safely arrived at the place of our destination, the place where we are able to pass some few of the next years of our life after a voyage of nearly eight months. It would be impossible for me to make you fully aware of the sensations I experienced on arrival with a mixture of anxiety, of fear, of joy, of hope as I never before felt. Our passage from the Cape was of the tedious length of eleven weeks which to me appeared insufferably long, as I had not the good fortune to enjoy my health, a severe attack of Pleurisy and Rheumatism confined me to my Room a long time and for some weeks to my cot, during which time I suffered much. As I am now quite recovered from the Complaint tho not quite restored to my strength, I should not, my ever dear Mother, have given you the pain of knowing this, had I not been certain that the great absence in my journal would have told the secret. I was however in the hands of a very attentive surgeon (Mr Carter of the 73rd) and you may suppose had as kind and attentive a nurse as was possible for a man to have. Eliza watched over me most assiduously, never left me and was one great means of my recovery. Thanks to her care, before we came to Port, I had quite overcome the complaint, and was rapidly getting my strength: but the Hot Season of the Year which we encountered at landing and the late and present wet weather retarded my complete rejuvenation of strength, which I have no doubt, the mildness and salubrity of the Winter in this climate will completely restore. We were 15 days after we first made the S.W Cape of Van Dieman's land before we entered the Harbour at Port Jackson. The wind was so light and the current set so strongly against us, that we were for three days within 40 miles of our destination and could never get up to it. This at the close of a long voyage, was, as you may well suppose, truly mortifying – and the last night of our being at sea was truly tremendous. We were within 4 miles of a Rocky coast obliged to lay to, the Wind blowing a Hurricane, the Rain falling in torrents. The thunder and lightening as I never before heard or saw. The ship rolling very heavily, the Cabins full of water, and our cot swinging vehemently against the sides of the ship that I thought the frame of it would be broken and ourselves dashed out. But next morning amply repaid us. At seven o'clock I went on the Quarter deck; the sky was serene the wind fresh and fair as could blow. The Hindostan with every yard of sail set leading us along the bold coast of NSW, about two miles from the entrance of Botany Bay. The water is very deep close to the shore, the shore itself is very low and sandy and the coast very barren and forbidding in its aspect. The entrance to Botany Bay is very singular like the entrance of large gates in the coach house yard. We saw numerous tribes of the Natives along the shore and about ½ past eight we distinctly saw the signal post on the south Head of Port Jackson. From Botany Bay to Port Jackson the Coast gradually becomes more bold and lofty precipes or Headlands white as the Culvor Cliffs, the two last of which form the entrance of the latter harbour. We now hoisted our English Flag, and shortly after shewed our numbers to the fort. Having got well off the entrance we fired a Gun as a signal for Pilots to come off to us. They were very shortly on board of us and by ten o'clock we dropt our anchors as the Wind was not favourable for carrying us up to Sydney Cove, within the Heads of Port Jackson. The Band which was on the Quarter Deck immediately struck up 'God save the King' which had a powerful effect upon all of us. This was on Thursday 28 December. We had hoped to have had our Xmas dinner on shore, but in this we were disappointed. How much I thought of you all! but if it makes you more comfortable to know we are living in the greatest comfort here. But I must proceed in making my narrative. Several persons came to visit us, or rather to pay their respects to the Governor on that day: amongst the Riot was Colonel Foveaux of the N.S. Wales Regiment who was at that time the real Governor of the Settlement tho Colonel Paterson was the nominal Lieutenant Governor, but the Health of this latter Gentleman was so bad, that all the duties of the Situation devolved upon Colonel Foveaux. He is a pleasant looking and handsome, tho' a very corpulent Man, quite a Man of business and extremely attentive and obliging. To him we are indebted for the comforts of a nice house and many other accommodations which his kindness procured for us and which we should certainly have wanted had it not been for him. From the different persons who came on board we learnt that Commodore Bligh was at the Derwent, waiting for assistance from home, but that the settlement was in the most perfect state of quiet and order, which we found to be the case. Colonel Foveaux sent us on board a reasonable supply of Poultry and fresh meat, which I in particular stood in need of. I was also able to get some Port Wine, which was very necessary for me, all the Captain's stock having been out for some time and nothing left but some bad Madeira which we drank from the Cask. This I durst not touch. Had I been able to get but one glass of Port a day after my disorder had left me, I should have regained my strength much sooner. How I have longed for a Glass of my Father's! We were detained within the Heads until Saturday, during which time we saw many visitors and did nothing but ask questions so incessantly, and importantly as hardly to wait for an answer.

The Harbour of Port Jackson is extremely pretty indeed. It has the appearance of being tolerably well wooded, branches into many sweet Coves, and is ornamented on its Banks, with small neat houses, which are extremely attractive. About 12 o'clock on Saturday 30 December a very slight Breeze sprang up in our favour; we shortly took advantage of it and about 4 o'clock cast anchor in Sydney Cove, in deep water tho not more than 50 yards from the Shore. The first appearance of the town on entering the Cove is very beautiful it is built in the form of a crescent round the Head of the Cove tho on entering the Town, It has no appearance of that form. The Government House is situated most delightfully on a neck of land, it is a charming object from the water. The Church is at a Convenience, and the hills above the town are crowned with Windmills which give the whole an appearance peculiarly English. The Absence of Bligh made Colonel Macquarie feel some difficulties respecting the opening of his commission. He sent for me, and made me acquainted with this difficulty at the same time shewing me his Instructions in which he was ordered to reinstate Governor Bligh for the space of 24 hours – he asked my advice told me that I was the only person he could consult except Colonel O'Connell the Lieutenant Governor. That he should do nothing of importance without my advice And should confide in me upon all occasions. I advised him to open his Commission and land the troops, as soon as possible, at the same time issuing a Proclamation declaratory of his instructions in regard to the late Governor, which proclamation I prepared and send to you No. 1 [included in original letter but not copied into this letterbook –Ed] He was quite delighted and I was at all in all with him. I have drawn up three other Proclamations equally to his satisfaction. Though this was the Secretary's duty. I did not choose to refuse it. He has appointed for his secretary a Mr Campbell, who was at the Head of the Discount Bank at the Cape of Good Hope, and who was recommended to him by Lord Caledon. Campbell is between 30 and 40, also in my opinion very fit for the situation, which is very troublesome, and only 10s per day. But this is exclusive of fees and it also must be considered that he is one of the Colonel's family, dining with him everyday, and dining wherever the Colonel is asked. The Colonel's Suite, then, consists of his Secretary, His Brigade Major, and his Aide de Camp, who attend him wherever he goes. On Sunday Morning, it being previously fixed, the Governor and Mrs Macquarie, Eliza and myself, with the Governor's Suite disembarked about 10 o'clock and entered the Boat which rowed us to the Government Wharf. The Yards of both Ships were manned by the Sailors in their best dress, who upon our boat leaving the ship's side, gave three cheers, immediately after both ships fired a Salute of 15 Guns, which upon our landing, was answered by the battery on shore. The Governor was received by Colonel Foveaux and the principal officers of the settlement while the N.S.Wales [Corps], was drawn up in two lines, from the Wharf to the Gates of the Governor's House. The Band was playing and the colours were flying, as we all moved through the lines the Officers saluted. The men were very clean but they are almost all old men. On arriving at Government House, which had been newly painted, and put into a complete state of repair, We found Colonel and Mrs Paterson, ready to receive the Governor. The Colonel, I have already observed, is very infirm indeed. He is a great Naturalist and an FRS. Mrs Paterson is a pleasant and obliging woman fat and forty, she is very sharp, knows her own interest very well and sticks to it, is a Scottish woman need I add a Woman of the World? Government House is very pleasantly situated and commands a charming view of the Cove and Town of Sydney. In the front of it there is a very excellent verandah, or covered way which shades the House very much. The entrance is into a tolerable Hall with one good room to the right which is the Governor's business room. On the left is the dining room. Through that is the drawing room, and through that the Governor and Mrs Macquarie's bed room, which has a dressing room behind it. Over these are some servant's rooms, and small bedrooms. The House has been built at different times and is therefore inconvenient. But the offices, kitchen etc which in this country is always detached are roomy and very convenient. The Garden and pleasure grounds are very good, and all is enclosed with a park paling. But much may yet be done in the way of improvement. After staying here some little time, Eliza, myself and Captain Pritchard and the Secretary went to call upon the late Judge Advocate, in order to see the House, in which as you may suppose we felt very much interested. About this too, you will expect me to be very particular. It is very near Government House, and the situation is extremely eligible indeed I would not change the situation for any other in Sydney. It stands rather high and has a very pretty view of the Cove towards which it fronts. Before the House is a very good garden full of Peach trees, apple trees etc in very bad order and surrounded with an old and extremely shabby paling. Behind the House is a very roomy yard, with a coach house both extremely decayed indeed and shabby. The yard was vilely dirty and both that, the garden, and the house showed they had belonged to an indigent and negligent master. The entrance door of the house is mean, narrow and shabby. It opens upon a Hall about 16 feet square, with a fire place in it which serves for a dining room. On the left is another room about 18 by 17, on the right is another of about the same dimensions. One of these rooms is on each side of the Hall. The windows are extremely insignificant and by no means proportioned to the height of the rooms which may be called lofty. Each room has a fire place. These three rooms may be called the only habitable part of the House which alas! is but one storey high. But adjoining to and behind these rooms there are what are called skillings in this country. These are mainly small rooms, the back wall of which is low, and the Roof shelving and meant merely for servants. Of these rooms which are in a miserable state, there were three: so that the whole house consisted of six rooms. There was a Back door opening upon the Yard, in which there is a detached kitchen, upon the point of tumbling down. When we called Mr Atkins was ill in Bed, so that we did not at that time see him. But we have since seen him. He is 63 years old and a very fine looking man, very prepossessing in his appearance, engaging and easy in his manners and sensible and pleasant in his conversation. He is quite A Gentleman in his deportment and plainly shews that he is in a situation beneath him and has been accustomed to the polished and higher classes of life. He has travelled a great deal. To set off against this, he is a most inordinate drinker of spirits when alone and is constantly intoxicated. But when in company he has never been known to exceed. For Colonel Foveaux dined in his company for seven months together, during the whole of which time he never seemed in the smallest degree intoxicated. He lost his wife a little before our arrival. She was not a woman of any taste I am sure. For the windows and doors were all bordered with low and vulgar caricatures, and the doors themselves painted with alternate colours of Blue and white. The furniture was very poor and very dirty, the House itself a perfect pigstye. Mr Atkins has three illegitimate daughters and an old housekeeper living with him of whom public opinion speaks nothing in their favour. While I am upon this subject I may as well add what is to be done to this ruin of a place. It has been found the walls are too weak to bear an upper storey, and the Governor, who says he has nothing so much at heart as our comfort thought at first of pulling it entirely down and building me a new house, two storeys high, at Government expence. This on the whole would have been the most economical and certainly the best plan, but in the present state of things it would have taken up a very long time accordingly upon a further examination it has been determined to add another wing to contain three good rooms and to build a new Kitchen and servants hall adjoining to it opposite the new Wing, according to the enclosed rough plan. In the mean time I have not been idle. Two of the Men who the Governor allows me are Gardeners, one of them is a very good one indeed sent purposely from the Hawkesbury country for me. As Mr Atkins has left the house, I allow this gardener to live in the kitchen, and both together have got the Garden into very nice order and have planted it with all kinds of vegetables such as Peas, Beans, Kidney Beans, broccoli, cabbage, turnips, radishes and potatoes in great abundance. There were already excellent asparagus beds there which I manured, cut and put into order so that I Have already had great plenty of fine asparagus as I ever saw in Convent Garden Market. I have put into my yard also, a dozen fowls, 18 geese, three turkies 6 ducks and a nice little Chinese sow in pig, which last was a present to me. The Government men put me up, anything I want, so that I got a stye, troughs, buckets, wheelbarrows, garden utensils from the stores at no expence. All the above animals are fat and fit to kill, and Eliza and myself regale upon a goose this very day.

But where you will say are you living in the mean time? This is a fortunate question and reminds me that I must leave you, my Dear Mother for the present and return to my narrative. On leaving this wreck of a place, I made up my mind for a further residence on board ship for at least a month for I thought that was the shortest time that it would take for Mr Atkins to leave it and for the Government to put it into tenantable repair. It was unpleasant, but I thought there was no help for it. Colonel Foveaux had invited us to dinner but we excused ourselves and returned on board to dinner. In the afternoon I was much surprised and pleased by a letter from the Governor saying that Colonel Foveaux had got a Mr Thompson to lend us his house ready furnished for such time as we wanted it and that it was now ready for our reception. Mr Thompson came out a convict to this country, but is now, I may say, one of the first men if not the first in the Colony. He possesses an amazing herd of cattle, a most extensive property at the Hawkesbury where he generally lives. Besides he has to the amount of £50,000 engaged in different pursuits. He has established a Tan yard where he manufactures leather from the skins of kangaroos and seals. He has also a Saltwork etc etc. He is a Bachelor and built the house at Sydney for his residence but has since determined to reside at the Hawkesbury where he has also a House. This intelligence was most joyfully accepted.

It having been agreed on, the Commissions should be read on the public parade on the following day and that I should administer the oaths, to the Governor next morning, Eliza and myself repaired after breakfast to government house. About 10 o'clock the whole of the 73rd Regiment was landed in excellent order and about 300 strong and marched to the Parade.– It was Monday, the first day in the new year. The morning was remarkably fine but excessively hot. About 12 o'clock the Governor and Mrs Macquarie, Eliza and myself went in the Governors carriage, which is but a chariot, to Colonel Foveaux on the Parade about a short mile from Government House. The 73rd and NS Wales Corps were drawn up in a square. After taking some refreshment there, we all went to the Middle of the Square. God save the King was struck. The troops fired a volley and there was a general discharge from the batteries and ships. The Colonel and myself were in the front of the Rest. The Aide de Camp then delivered the Governor his Commission, the Governor took it out of the box, shewed the Great Seal to me and at the same time presented the Commission to me which I received with my Hat off. I then unfolded the Commission upon which a General Volley was fired and all were uncovered. I immediately began to read the Commission. It took up 20 minutes being on these broad skins of parchment. During the time an orderly Sergeant held an umbrella over me, to defend my face and bald head from the sun. I afterwards read the Lieutenant Governor's and my own. The Governor then made a suitable speech and the whole was concluded by three general volleys. That Day we dined at Colonel Foveaux's with the Governor and were elegantly entertained. The 73rd marched off the Parade to their encampment about three miles from the town.

In the evening we slept for the first time in New South Wales in the house that was provided for us, and thought ourselves very lucky having as good a house on shore so soon. The house is I assure you one of the prettiest in Sydney. The entrance is into a very good hall – having on each side of it a room of 17 feet square – on the same floor there is also a butler's pantry. Upstairs there are two good bedrooms, one of which is the nursery and three servants bedrooms and a good storeroom. There is a charming verandah both above and below. There are also extremely good cellars. The kitchen is not yet built but there is a small wooden house close to this and within the gates which serves that purpose very well.

This then is the place which we at present inhabit, and which we have I assure you made very comfortable. The House was only just finished, but in many of its requisites it was incomplete. It is not above 100 yards from the Head of the Cove, to which, as well as the street it was entirely open. This was extremely inconvenient as the Natives quite naked would come up to the very windows of the house. But Colonel Foveaux who supervised the works, enclosed me a yard of good size towards the Cove with a six foot cedar paling so that we are now quite secured. Indeed tho' this place abounds in desperate characters, we never had reason to apprehend any thing from them for I have an armed constable in constant attendance about the house night and day – who is regularly relieved at certain intervals. This is my privilege ex officio, and this is a very comfortable one. For in the day time I employ him upon such messages as we have occasion to send and in other odd jobs and in the night he takes care that no idle fellows come within a hundred yards of the house. I forgot to observe that after the parade we adjourned to Government House where before a considerable assemblage I administered the oath to the Governor and he afterwards administered them to the Lieutenant Governor and myself. After this the Governor gave the Proclamation to his Secretary who read it aloud, to the great astonishment of some of them, I have no doubt. And thus ended the business of the day which fatigued me exceedingly.

On the 7 of January H.M.S Porpoise came into Harbour with Commodore Bligh on Board from the Derwent, a settlement on the South Coast of Van Dieman's Land. The Porpoise to our utmost delight brought us letters from England and Papers which it had received from the Albion, Private Vessel from London, which had arrived at the Derwent after a remarkably quick passage of four Months. How do I thank you my Dearest Mother for your interesting letter. I read it over and over again and keep it by me as a source of satisfaction to me! But I must not revert to it at present. The next day Commodore Bligh and his daughter Mrs Putland landed with great ceremony, amid the salutes of the Ships and Batteries. He was received by a detachment of the 73rd Regiment and proceeded to Government House. He is a broad stout little man, past the Prime of Life considerably. His daughter married a Captain Putland a Commander in the

Navy upon the N.S.Wales station, who is since dead. His widow, is about 26, rather pretty but extremely affected and proud. God knows of what! Her temper is as evident as that of her father and that is more violent than I could have conceived. They are a pretty pair and I cordially wish they were in England, for he is eternally troubling me. He is revengeful in the extreme and I'm sure would be delighted to hang draw and quarter all those who deprived him of his Government. I have had a regular official correspondence with him. He hoists his flag on board the Hindostan, in which his daughter returns to England, in which he takes with him all the principal officers of the civil department there, as evidences on certain charges he means to exhibit against Colonel Johnston.

About 12 on the same day, the Governor, Mrs Macquarie, the Commodore in one carriage and Mrs Putland, Eliza, myself and Mr Griffin the Commodore's Secretary in Mr Campbell's coach and four, went to Camp to see the 73rd through some manoeuvres and first in compliment to the Queen. The Camp is in a pretty situation, but the road to it is very bad, such as you would not venture to go through on any account. We returned and dined at Government House. These are the only interesting points if they can be called so, since our arrival. I have not been able to keep a journal, for my time is very much taken up. It is not now as when I was on board ship. We are also a good deal occupied in getting our Furniture ready and I am sure that you will be pleased to hear that my Profits upon a small quantity I bought at Rio and upon some Wine I bought at the Cape, will pay for the furnishing of my House. For 57 gallons of brandy which cost me £17.2s I have got £142.10 and for a Pipe of Cape Wine which cost me £20 I can get £120, whenever I like. I also bought at Rio a quantity of Cocoa, Coffee, Rice and Candles for my domestic purposes, all of which things are dear here, and often not to be had and some tobacco which I shall dispose of to my advantage. I luckily bought some Tea from the Cape which at our arrival here was selling at £2.2 per lb. – tho now in consequence of arrivals from China and India, It is not more than eight shillings at the very best. The rest of my letter will be taken up, first in giving you some accounts of this place, its society, the mode and expence of living next of our own domestic Establishment and the manner in which we live; and next I shall revert to your letter from home. First, as to the Country, on this point I cannot say very much, as I have not been further into it than the Camp, which is about three miles from Sydney and I shall not trouble you with what I can collect from others, as I shall no doubt have an opportunity of giving you my ideas upon it from actual observations of my own. One thing however is necessary to share, before you can be aware of the situation of this Colony. For its consumption of flour and bread, it depends entirely on the settlement of the Hawkesbury, which is about 40 miles from Sydney and is in a district of land of the most amazing fertility extending for upwards of 60 miles along the River of that name. But the River generally overflows into its banks every year, and the flood carries away everything with it. And on the other hand, if the wheat escapes the Flood, the quantity is generally so great that the farmer is generally ruined by its cheapness, there being no market for the surplus produced. There was just before our arrival, the greatest flood of the Hawkesbury ever known. The river rose in a most sudden manner to the height of 75 feet above its usual level, and swept before it Sheep, Pigs, farms, houses in short everything. In consequence of this flood therefore there was a great scarcity when we came into the country and bread was at a most extravagant price a small loaf weighing two pounds being sold at 1s 6d. Indeed about all articles are here very dear, or very cheap – for on account of the Colony being at so great a distance from the Mother Country, and from other countries which might furnish supplies, the market is either overstocked to a great account, or completely empty. For instance tea, will sometimes sell at 5 guineas a Pound and the next week with the arrival of a China ship will reduce the price to so many shillings. You will therefore, my sweet Mother, see the necessity in this Country of buying in large stocks of such things as are daily used, such as Sugar, Tea, Soap, candles etc for unless that is done you might be reduced to the necessity of foregoing entirely such things as habit almost entirely rendered necessary or else of paying most extravagant prices for them. The Products of this country are very good indeed. All kinds of kitchen vegetables grow in great perfection here and may be had in every month of the year. The Apricots and peaches are of remarkable beauty and flavour. The peas are both superior in size and delicacy than any I ever saw in England. They are too in great plenty. Nectarines are most common here, and Grapes do not *come to much perfection for the cultivation of them is much neglected and little understood. I do not think the apples as good, by any means as those in England. But the Quinces, figs and mulberries are singularly fine. Gooseberries and currants will not grow here, at all, for the climate is not cold enough. The Water Melon grows here to the most astonishing size, I dare to say three times the bigness of a Head, and is of very fine flavour indeed. All these fruits are very cheap – I have fed my pig with peaches. The Strawberry and Raspberry are both fine in this country. The Beef and Mutton here are as good as those in England. Veal is here very scarce, as calves are seldom if ever killed for the market. Lamb and Pork are both excellent. The Poultry of all sorts are very fine. Turkies I have seen equal to those of Norfolk. The Wild Duck and Teal of this country are very superior too. With respect to fish, there is a great falling off. The finest we have is the Whiting, and the Rock Cod, which is very different from the fish so called which is caught on the Coast of Ireland. Oysters are plentiful. There are two sorts; the Rock oyster which is very small and good, somewhat like the Colchester and the land oyster, which is large, coarse and much inferior. There are not any lobsters; but the crawfish are very large and good. By this you will find that on the whole, living is here very good, and good dinners, ay, such as an Alderman would wish, may be obtained. But the Mischief of all in this is that everything here is very good, it is extremely dear. Beef, mutton, pork, and lamb are each 1s 6d per lb and all parts are charged at the same price, rough and smooth coarse and fine, so that the first comer is the best served. Fowls fit for the table are 6d or 8d the couple. A fat Turkey, £1 a fat goose 10s a fat duck 5s per pound and often 6s. The price of what is called here a good milk cow may be £20 – but the cows of this country go dry very soon and it is well known that one English cow will give more milk than six native cows. The average price on Saturday March 3rd as appears by the accounts officially given me by the clerk of the market of wheat was 16s 5d oats and maize each 8d, Barley 9s per bushel. Potatoes 13s 6d per lb.*

The common people of this country are the most immoral set I ever met with. The Women constantly live with the men in a state of prostitution, and openly avow it. To use their own words 'it is the Fashion of the country and few think of marrying'. Spirits they will buy at any price and some men will drink out £100 in less than three days. They think nothing of giving 5s for a glass of brandy. Till the time of the present Governor, Sunday was the same as any other day, and work and labour regularly went on. But I must reserve this subject for another opportunity. There is a great plenty of very good necessaries but the dearness of labour makes everything else dear. Furniture is accordingly very expensive. The wood, generally used is that of the cedar, which tho' coarse somewhat resembles the mahogany. The best wood is very pretty but it is very hard, and will not stand in the solid and is therefore used only in veneering. For a chest of drawers you might pay £15. The town of Sydney is often irregularly built no plan seems to have been attended to, and no Judgement exerted. The houses, in general consist of only one storey; tho' some few of the inhabitants have built handsome ones. Mr Lord's, is a very good one built of stone three storeys high. Those of Mr Underwood and Mr Campbell and Merchant and Naval Officers here, are also very great. There is too a neat orphan school. But it must be remarked that all these are private buildings. The only decent public building is the Church and that is nothing extraordinary. It may well be said that the Government at home and the Government here have done nothing for the Colony. There is not even a Court House for the purpose of Justice. All the houses here have a little garden annexed to them, which finds the whole a pretty appearance and makes the town cover a great deal of ground and the houses be very airy. But there is not a street that can be called handsome. Yet every stranger coming here is astonished that such a place could arise in twenty years. The Society here consists almost exclusively of the Wives of the Officers of the 102nd and 73rd Regiments. Mrs Paterson I have already mentioned.We are very intimate with her. Mrs Abbott, wife of Major Abbott of the 102nd we also know. She is a very good kind of a woman. But I know of none worthy of extraordinary mention. It is impossible to say anything else of them than they are of the common run, neither good, bad or indifferent; so that the whole Bunch of them can not furnish matter to fill six lines of a letter. The Climate of this country is supposed to be very fine, and everybody here speaks highly of it. The whole of January was very hot in the Sun, but the Sea breeze is very pleasant and moderates the heat exceedingly. But it is necessary to avoid exposure to the sun. The Thunder and Lightening is tremendous.

We had a very heavy storm, the Saturday after we arrived. It was indeed awful. The Peals are sometimes like the burst of an immense cannon close to the ear; at other times are very long and crashing; the lightening at the same time flashing vividly. I have seen seven flashes of lightening during one peal of thunder, each time the sky appearing to open the whole length of the flash. February was very rainy and this month seems likely to seem so too. The Maize or Indian Corn Harvest will be in this month. For there are two harvests in a year, one of maize and one of wheat. The ensuing harvest is likely to be a very good one, if a flood should not come but that is rather apprehended from the quantity of rain that has fallen. It rains surprisingly heavy in these hot climates, and continues sometimes for two or three days together. The Disorder most prevalent here is the Dysentery, which is general owing to intemperate living or eating excessively of fruit. By common care and prudence, it may be avoided. But when it comes, it generally puts an end to the poor patient in three days. The late Judge Advocate is now so ill with it that he is not expected to recover. Lunacy is also common, and inflammations of the eyes. Now for ourselves. Eliza is very well, and much pleased with this country because she found it much better than she expected. She was at first, as you may [imagine], very busy in unpacking and putting everything in order. Everything came very well, but the Box containing our plated things and knives forks etc. Unfortunately the salt water got to it, and has completely spoiled our whole stock six dozen of knives and forks. They were almost all eaten through by Rust; we had all ground but it has not done them any good, the Rust had eaten so deeply into them. The Chamber candlesticks were also spoiled, and also the steel snifters. But the cooking and glass came quite safe, not a Plate nor Glass were broken. The box of linen, which you my dear mother, so kindly packed and gave us, I unpacked with my own hands. I found it exactly as you had left it, it was as smooth, and as dry as if it had not been packed an hour. It put me in mind of you. I kissed the check furniture[1] which was at the top, over and over. – my books also came very safely. Everything in short, came safely and in good condition, other than that one box. I have already told you my dear Mother that we have two good rooms, below stairs, one of which is the sitting room is now nearly furnished with our furniture, indeed entirely except the sofa. We have on the floor a small Wilton carpet. There is also a good Glass, a Dozen very neat new Cedar Chairs with India cane bottoms, a Rembroke table of cedar and two other Tables. And I must add, that the room is the picture of cleanliness. Any Person might eat of the floor. Eliza is the nicest creature possible, and cannot bear anything either dirty or disorderly. The other room I made my study and as the eating room. We have in it a plain, neat set of dining tables, that will dine a dozen persons very comfortably, a cellonet, two bookcases put up by Government for my Books – a Carpet not very good which Major Abbott gave us and a Secretary bookcase for my private papers, on which I am this moment writing. There is unfortunately in each of these rooms four windows – but as we are not settled here for good we have not curtains. I am sure these two rooms are the neatest in the colony, certainly the cleanest. The Governor's tho' larger are not kept half so nice. They are quite comfortable. Up stairs there are two good Bedrooms to the back one, of which we occupy. The other is a nursery. In our bedroom there is a fourpost bed of Mr Thompson's; the chairs are also his. But we have two chests of drawers of our own. There are two windows in the Room looking upon the Cove, and the opposite side of the town of Sydney. It is also very comfortable. The Nursery is nearly the same except there is another room, behind it with a door between them, which Eliza uses as a store room. The child sleeps still with Elizabeth, but we mean to have either a cot or a crib for him. There are also Three bedrooms for servants. Our establishment consists of Elizabeth who takes care of the child and gets up Eliza's dresses etc. Little Ellis who is now a charming boy runs about all day long, is the delight of his mother and mine also, and lively and entertaining beyond anything. Nothing escapes his notice. If there is the least alteration in the room he observes it – laughs and looks at me, goes up to it and holds up his little hands and cries oh pretty, pretty! He can say mama very well and sometimes papa; but that is the limit of his speechifying. He does not care, much, about toys. He breaks them in a minute and never minds them. But he is very fond of looking at a book, and turning over the leaves of it. He is very well and fat; But since he has come one of his eyes has been very bad; and we were obliged to have it blistered.[2]_He cuts his teeth very well and has already some double ones. He is always in mischief has perpetual accidents by falls, but he soon forgets them. He is one of the most proportionate creatures I ever saw and I'm quite sure will require a good deal of checking ere' long.

Elizabeth is not so useful as she might be – for she is full of vanity and conceit and thinks of nothing but dress, on which she spends all the little money she has. I wish she was in England for she is a very expensive servant to us. We give her £20 pr annum and fund her in tea and sugar also. Living on board ship so long a time and the notions that were put into her head at the Cape have spoiled her. She is restless and discontented into the Bargain, tho' she has high wages, and nothing to do. We have also a young girl, a settler's daughter at the Hawkesbury, which are the only decent kind of servant to get. For all the women in Sydney have some improper connexion or other. She acts as Housemaid and does anything she is desired. Besides she is an excellent needlewoman and we have every reason to be pleased with her. We furnish her with clothes and her meat and drink but pay her no wages. We have also a Man and his wife whom we found on the premises as servants to Mrs Thompson, whom we now employ, Mr Thompson having now given them up to us. But they are not cheap servants. Both together will cost £36 per annum. They are too constantly quarrelling but it is so difficult to meet with even tolerable Servants here, that we are obliged to submit to these things, for if we were to change them, we should probably get ten times worse. She is a very good Cook indeed for our purposes and can get a dinner very well but she is intolerably violent in her temper. Joseph, her husband, is an excellent footman, very willing, quick, active, sober and honest too. He waits at Table very well, and cleans up his things and does his work. The first servant I had was a soldier but he was lazy, idle, slow and did nothing but smoke and drink we were obliged to send him back to his duty. I have also a Man allowed me by Government, whom I employ in cutting wood, fetching water, feeding my fowls and any other jobs I want done. But as the Government Servants work only till three o'clock in the day and never on Saturdays or Sundays. I allow him to eat with the Servants and to sleep in one of the uninhabited houses on condition of his giving into the general stock his rations and working at all times and days when called upon. He is an Irishman and one of the most hardworking fellows

I ever saw. George also lives in the house, but he is upon the stores and finds his own clothes and washing. The Cook washes her own and her husband's clothes; and the rest of the washing is done at a very reasonable rate £40 per annum. It is otherwise 4s per dozen, great and small, which comes very high indeed as much as £1.8 per week, which you know is considerably more than the above annual Price. Eliza, the little boy, George and myself are upon the stores, in consequence of this we have 21lbs of fresh beef pr week and a considerable quantity of wheat. The Beef is excellent being much superior to that which comes from the Butcher's and they always let me have what part I want on sending a little before hand to the stores. The Wheat is very moderate and I have hitherto used it, for my Poultry, but when the Maize comes in I shall send it to the Baker's who will give me a certain quantity of Bread for it. Eliza has a Baker's Book, and a Butcher's book and a Ration Book which is taken to each respectively when we want anything, and the quantity put down, and she pays the Bill every Monday morning. Our Butter and Milk, we get from the same person, a Mr Blaxland a settler in this colony and settle the same way. The servants here are of course allowed either Butter or Cheese and nothing to drink but water. We actually breakfast at eight o'clock, dine at four – drink tea at 8 – and find no necessity for taking lunch and Supper. The servants dine at one o'clock. We have already had one formal party. It consisted of Colonel and Mrs Paterson, Colonel Foveaux, Mr Finucane his secretary – Captain Duser – Captain Porteous of H.M.S Porpoise, Major and Mrs Scott – Mr Pritchard and Mr Carter, Surgeon of the 73rd Regiment. We sat down 12 – to a Boiled leg of lamb, suckling pig, Roast beef, curried Fowl, Mutton Harico, boiled fowls and vegetables – Roast Duck – asparagus – green peas and Sweets in a Second Course – all judiciously disposed of. It was too hot for soup – and the People who have been here long have great contempt for the fish here. The dinner well dressed – and Joseph alone waited remarkably well. He is himself a good cook and understands putting a dinner on the Table. But unfortunately our best set was found so deficient that we were obliged to borrow another. There are by no means dishes enough nor large enough. There is no soup Tureen etc. But it will do pretty well for about eight persons. In this country they give very large crowded dinners – which I own I am surprised at, as they only increase one's sense of the Heat of the Climate. The Governor here lives very well, sees a good deal of company and is very hospitable. We are upon the best terms, and we have dined there several times, indeed, we were the first persons he saw at his Table – Eliza is a very good housekeeper and clean and neat, I assure you, I believe there is no waste here and as little expense. We live in a plain, neat manner as economical as we can. We are both, I hope too sensible and proud not, to see, the folly of living ostentatiously. But yet, I have no doubt that my expenses will exceed the Governor in mere housekeeping. He has everything found for him – As much meat as he chuses – a boat employed constantly in fishing for him – Parramatta supplies him with milk, butter, poultry, vegetables etc etc – In short he has no expence but Wine, and grocery, which always came out freight free to him – and reasonable in price. Government Men make for him what furniture he pleases – if he wishes for any alterations in his house; to build, to pull down, it costs him nothing. The house is nearly furnished with Government furniture, and what is wanting he can supply free of cost. Horses are kept and found for him. In short it is a most excellent situation for he is absolute Master: He can do what he likes and no one can say him 'Nay' – I have endeavoured, my dear Mother, as far as I can, to give you an accurate idea of our situation. I have felt that I was answering you, and therefore have been very minute and precise. Some things may have escaped, if so, they shall form the subject of any letter – which I shall very soon have an opportunity of writing. For an account of my official duties I must refer you to my letter to Jeffery, which I send by this same conveyance. Viz. the Brig Experiment (Dodds Master) under the cover of Colonel Foveaux.

Thursday March 8. About 4pm yesterday the alarm was given that the Dromedary was on fire. Thick Smoke was seen issuing in volumes from the Port Holes. The alarm turned out true. Very fortunately the powder was on shore; except a small quantity which was soon removed. The spot where the fire was could not be discovered on account of the thick smoke; so that about 8 o'clock they were obliged to cut her cables tow her on shore and scuttle her. About ten the Ship had ten feet of water in her hold and the fire was completely extinguished. It was supposed to have begun in the spirit room by a bit of Candle having been carelessly left among some brooms there. No lives were lost – and the damage sustained is principally in the key stores and slops. If she had been blown up, I think our house must have been blown down. Thank God. It is so well over. You have no idea. My dearest Mother how delighted we were on hearing a ship had entered the Port, with letters from England. It was H.M.S Porpoise from the Derwent with Commodore Bligh on board. Previous to her departure from thence, the Albion South Whaler, had arrived there in four months from the Lizard Point; and had brought letters from England which the Porpoise brought to us. I was indeed pleased with the kind mark of your affection and regard for the poor exile from his country, evinced in so long and interesting a letter … Here as far as the necessaries and comforts of life can make us so, we are comfortable. I feel that I am respected here by everybody, that everybody looks up to me, that I have already gained a character for abilities and integrity. To use your own expression time and Reflection will I trust reconcile you to this temporary separation. Eliza feels very sensibly your kindness, my dear Mother, in sending her the Border you worked on and sent to her, which has been safely received. She is making a gown for it, which I shall admire more than any other she has – and she will wear it on my Birthday which is now at hand. I have just given orders for a writing desk to be made here out of the best wood of this country, which I shall request your acceptance of in return for yours which I am now writing upon. I hope to be able to send it by Colonel Paterson in the Dromedary when she is ready. But the workmen are here very dilatory … Porter, port wine and Madeira are the principal things I shall want, I am in great hopes, that my fees here will be fully adequate to my expences.

I feel much sorrow for poor Mr Clarke's family – it was indeed fortunate they did not fail before when they had so much money of mine in their hands … I wrote from Madeira, from Rio and from the Cape, long letters to you, accompanying my Journals and accounts of Madeira, Porto Praya and Rio. What Journal I have remaining I shall send by the next opportunity, but my illness renders it more defective than it would have been otherwise. I am happy you received the letter and Journals I sent in by the Prize, and that you were gratified by them. I trust my others will be equally satisfactory. I have received by the Ann which arrived a few *days ago in perfect safety, a charming voyage, a letter from Mr Coutts the Banker, covering one from Lord Northland and one of recommendation from Mr Coutts to the Governor. I feel very grateful to Lord Northland for his kind interference, and shall have pleasure in acknowledging his letter and employing so respectable a house as that of Coutts, I send by this opportunity the Sydney Gazettes as low as I can get them and the different proclamations.*

Sydney 9 March 1810
My Dearest Jeffery,

... I was most unfortunately attacked at once by both acute Rheumatism and pleurisy which confined me to my cot for some time – and to my cabin for nearly the whole of this last period of the voyage I had blisters all over me there at a time and lost in one week 60 ounces of blood. This has occasioned a debility which I have not even yet got over – for in addition to this my only food for a long time was barley water and sago without any wine in it ... the town of Sydney is really wonderful. There are several very good private houses. The town is very large, larger than the Cape and at present abundantly supplied with everything ... The Climate is excellent and tho the thermometer in the Summer rises very high, yet the Heat is not felt so inconvenient as in England because during the heats all persons keep themselves quiet, and never venture in the sun more than is absolutely necessary. Tho' we have had some very wet weather, I have not once found it oppressive to me. The greatest nuisances, I know, are the flies; which are numerous and tormenting, beyond conception. I do not mean mosquitos for those are confined to the woods, but the Common flies. Some of them will absolutely blow the meat, while it is on your plate, and in a moment it is covered with maggots. The Natives, are the most ugly savage set I ever saw, they are miserably poor and have the appearance of being half famished. They are the lowest in the scale of human existence many being very little superior to baboons. They are, as you may suppose the most tormenting Beggars

possible and very expert thieves. They prefer spirits (every kind of which they call Rum) to anything. They are very common in the Town, everyday there are numbers of them, and almost all of them speak English very well. Bennellong who Collins has mistakenly stated to be dead, is alive, and has paid me several visits, but I take no notice of him. I should constantly have him about my house: and when you encourage them they are very difficult to be got rid of. One day A Chief of the name of Bungaree paid me a visit. He had his spears with him, which I desired him to throw. He threw one with astonishing dexterity and force hitting the object he aimed at, at a distance of at least 100 yards. I gave him a cup of Red Wine – on which he said – No Rum! Him like Rum better. He drank it off, then tapped his black belly and said – 'was good – was very good – but him like Rum better'. But my Dear Jeffery, I must postpone, to another opportunity all further description of these Men, and of the Country... This letter I shall devote in a great measure to giving you as ample and accurate an account of my official situation, its duties and its emoluments as possible. Indeed my dear Jeffery the Situation I have undertaken is very arduous and troublesome as it is at present constituted and one of great responsibility. I have no one whatever to give me assistance, or competent to advise me on any question of law. I have found everything in my department in the utmost confusion, and that all law business has been done in the most slovenly irregular, illegal manner conceivable; the Courts of Civil and Criminal Jurisdiction are Courts of Record. But there are no criminal records to be found and what few records of a civil nature there may be are imperfect and unintelligible. All the orders of the Court have been verbal orders. All Commitments are verbal. There are no such things as Declarations, Pleas etc. Everything has been done in a summary manner. Indeed the Patent orders that all disputes shall be decided in a Summary manner. All Debts above £300, are considered as debts of Honour – for tho' the case be perfectly clear, the Defendant when the Judgement of the Court is against him, appeals to the Governor and from him, to the Privy Council, the expence of which in usual obliges the Plaintiff to desist from any further suit. But now for my particular avocations. First of all as a Justice of the Peace I hear all complaints that are brought before me, and do all other acts usually done by a Justice of the Peace in England. In this Department, I am sadly pestered. Does anybody owe another money and he cannot regain it, a memorial and complaint is instantly made to me – and they are sadly disappointed when I refer them to the Civil Court. People also knowing that I am a Barrister constantly come in for my advice but no Fee is in their hands. A Bench of Magistrates is regularly held twice a week (on Tuesdays and Saturdays) at which I preside. All persons committed, in Gaol, are brought before us for examination. I take the examination down in the Bench Book, the Party is either discharged, punished, or remanded to prison to take his trial before a Criminal Court. The Bench Book is afterwards sent up to the Governor for his Inspection. The Bench then hear such Complaints as are brought forward by Prisoners and others against each other. The Bench till my time had assumed itself the cognizance of small debts, and decided upon hearing the parties themselves but I guide myself by the Patent which expressly declares that all pleas of debt and all personal pleas shall be decided by the Civil Court. I therefore refuse when on a Bench, to hear any complaint that is not of a Criminal nature. The Bench also every Saturday fix the Assize of Bread. On other days I am sufficiently employed by granting writs, taking affidavits, having examinations, discharging Bail Bonds etc etc – I also grant Probates and Wills, and letters of administration. The office Hours are from nine till three, but attendance is generally given till a later hour. All Agreements, transfers, Protests, Leases etc must be drawn by me and registered in my office. And there is something of this kind constantly in this office. I also draw all Precepts for an appointment of all coroners, Justices of the Peace, Constables etc etc and swear them into office. In a criminal court I exhibit and prepare all informations against prisoners – and record the Proceedings in civil courts – The first person I tried was Sir H. Brown Hayes, (before a Bench) for speaking insolently of Colonel Foveaux, and endeavoring to raise a riot. I reprimanded and discharged him. Since which he has sent me two Water melons every week, of uncommon size and goodness. He is a gentlemanly man, in his manners, tho' very odd in his dress and appearance. He has made a vow never to cut the hair on his upper lip, which is very long and gives him a very formidable and grave appearance. Hitherto there has not been a Criminal or a Civil court in my time. But on Monday next (today is Friday) there is to be a Criminal Court and on the Monday following a Civil Court. At the former there are to be here twenty prisoners tried for offences of different descriptions. I have not one information got made out for my Mother's letter has occupied me all the week and I have more to write and the ship sails on Sunday. I shall sit in my Gown and Wig for the first time for I did not choose to make it too common. For the Civil Court I Have issued upwards of 150 writs, to the amount I should think upwards of £50,000. Some of them have however been settled. The trying of these actions will give me an immense deal of trouble – for there are neither Attornies nor pleadings, nothing to define the specific course of action, and to prevent parties themselves from entering into desultory statements. And then the parties themselves are never satisfied and always think they must be right. So that I expect the next two or three weeks will be fully occupied. I imagine I have now told you all my avocations strictly of an official nature. It would be useless mentioning everything. Persons, I dare say twenty call every day upon trifling business, or for advice. Besides that I am liable to be sent for everyday to Government House if the Government wishes to consult me. I have had a long official correspondence with Governor Bligh respecting the witnesses he wishes to take home to substantiate certain charges against Governor Johnston etc and also respecting prosecutions he wishes to commence here against certain settlers. He is a most troublesome revengeful unpleasant man. I would he were out of the Colony!! I gave it as my opinion, that the facts could not amount to the legal charge of High Treason because they are not committed within the Realm of England (vide East) for the only Branch of High Treason they could possibly come under is a constructive levying of war against the King, which must be within the Realm. I will some time or other transmit a copy of the correspondence. Now for the emoluments of my Office and at first in regard to Actions, I take no fees upon any writ or affidavit whatever: and the only Emolument that arises to me from this Head, is in case an Appeal should be commenced, they must come to me for a Copy of the Proceedings upon which I charge at my discretion. Upon this Branch, therefore, I cannot form a Judgement, as no Civil Court has been held. And it has usually produced Atkins a good deal. 2nd For every grant of a Probate or Will or of letters of administration I receive four pounds and this is a very lucrative part of my fees and attended with very little trouble. 3rd Upon every agreement, transfer, lease etc and for registering the same I receive one Guinea which is small enough, God knows! When things are more settled this Branch will increase considerably. 4. I act as Notary Public and charge three Guineas for the smallest Protest done by the Master of a ship and something trifling for noting bills of exchange etc. The most troublesome business is that of making out Writs or Capias and affidavits, for which I get nothing. But it shall not be so long. Upon all these my clerk gets a shilling each … I keep a regular account of everything so that I can know at any moment the amount of fees received. As my own state of Health requires me to abstain from writing too much, and as George is perfectly ignorant of law business, I continue Mr Atkin's clerk in the office. He is an Irishman of the name of Fleming transported here for passing a forged note. He was a regular practicing Attorney, very well conversant in common conveyancing drawing Bail Bonds and in all the usual forms. He is very attentive and quick and saves me a vast deal of trouble. I believe him to be very honest in point of his dealings with me. But at night he is too apt to drink and be indecorous in the street, which I am sometimes obliged to take notice of. He is victualled from the stores and for further recompense I give him the Clerk's Fees which are very ample, I dare say equal to £100 pr annum. As it is, principally on account of George's ignorance I employ him, it is but fair George pay for it who gets his salary at £80 for nothing. George, however, is attentive, but not quick – and tho he can never make himself so useful as Fleming, he will do pretty well in town. But he is lethargic, has no Zeal about him and does not look sufficiently forward, and take pains to improve himself. Provided he has his belly filled, he cares for little else. I have certainly been deceived on him in several respects and especially in regard to his talents, which are not by any means great. He is on the contrary rather stupid. – I do expect the fees will answer all my expences here.

Mr Atkins at one time told me his fees amounted to £600 pr annum and at another £400 p annum. Mr Fleming used to account with him every Fortnight and has shewn me several distinct accounts, wherein the money received each fortnight amounted to more than £50 but whether these were at particular seasons, I do not know, or for extraordinary occasions. I rather think they arose principally from Appeals. I think I have now given you as full an account of these circumstances as I am able. One thing more, I must mention, namely the mode of payment in this country. There are four modes, viz. the notes drawn by the Paymasters of the different Regiments, for the subsistence of the troops, which notes are as low as 2s 6d each or 5s or 10s, or £1; £1.15; £2 and £5. It is necessary to draw these for all these different sums in consequence of the want of dollars. The Holders of these notes take them to the paymaster's every Quarter day and on giving them up receive in return, sets of Bills for the amount upon the Treasury. On this account they are almost always at a premium. The second mode is this – when any persons deliver Beef, corn, flour etc into the stores of the King, they receive receipts for the Quantity delivered in, at the fixed price, which are signed, by the Storekeeper and are called Store Receipts. These pass current for their amount, and are considered as good as Paynotes because they also on every Quarter day are consolidated in like manner by Bills on the Treasury, on being presented to the Commissary. Only the Bills drawn by the Commissary are at 90 days sight, while those drawn by the paymasters are at 30 days sight. The next mode of payment is in copper coin. The Farthing being current here for a Half penny that for a Penny also. Six shillings currency may be got for dollars. I now speak of the currency – everybody here issues promissory notes for any amount from 2.6d to £5 or more; and as it is impossible to tell which are bad or which are good (as every Blackguard even tho' he cannot write issues them) they are in great discredit and at very great discount. I have made an order that no payment whatever shall be taken at my office, but paynotes and store receipts, copper coins and dollars at 6d each and as persons must have their law business done I find the money comes in all the same, by which I not only secure myself from loss, but go to Market with great advantage. Thus my dear Jeffery, you will probably think with me, that my time is fully occupied from morn till night, and will be moreso while I am engaged in making those regulations I think absolutely necessary. It gives me much pleasure that I am likely to be appointed Judge of the Admiralty etc.

The articles I bought at Rio and the Cape I sold to much advantage as to pay with the profits the expence of my furniture ... This I speculated upon, and it has proved very lucky. I am very sorry [for] poor Clark the

Banker and very sorry for his family – God knows I wished him no harm. I wish to say a few words in respect to the choice of a Banker for me. By the Ann which arrived here a few days ago I received a letter from Mr Coutts the Banker covering a letter of recommendation from that Gentleman to the Governor in my favour, and one from Lord Northland to me. It appears that Lord Northland actuated by his kindness for me had prevailed on Mr Coutts to write this letter of recommendation and had also represented to him my misfortune with the failure of my Banker – at which Mr Coutts writes to me offering his Services and those of his House to me to secure my dividend from the Banker and also to be my agent and Banker in his letter to the Governor he desires him to tell me he charges nothing for Agency. On these accounts I should wish if you are not already engaged that you should deposit my money in the hands of Coutts and Co. as I think it may be of use to me and to you also: It certainly I should think would be much pleasanter than banking with those who are strangers to both of us.

So Moulsey is at length sold – Poor Dear Moulsey – I have often spent many happy hours in its lawns and its fields – and my present home and situation recall them to my memory with such force! But I must avoid these subjects. The Place of Kings Advocate at the Cape is as you know precarious in its Emoluments – and the Cape is dreadfully expensive. I do not think you could have got much even at present and a peace would certainly ruin you. I received all your letters, Storks, Eliot's my Mothers and Bessey's by Hulk S. Porpoise which received them from the Albion at the Derwent in 4 months from England. But I was a little disappointed in not receiving any from the Ann. I thank you for the Monthly and the Edinburgh and the Newspapers. The Ann was overtaken at Rio, by another ship bound here, which will I hope bring letters to us and brings us intelligence of a duel between Lord Castlereagh and Mr Canning and a consequent change of ministry. But we know no particulars. We have also heard of Lord Wellington's useless victory in Spain.

Pray send me La belle Assemblu, or more fashionable nonsense of that kind for Eliza. The Monthly is almost too dull even for me. I am sorry Holbourn has my poems and I hope he will not put my name to them.

God knows what trash he may talk to them and mine are of themselves bad enough. I wish Eliot had them. I send Sydney Gazettes which will tell you a little news. A vessel has just come in from New Zealand and brings account of the New Zealanders having burnt the ship Boyd (lately from Ireland with convicts) and slain all the Crew.[3] This is rather awkward news, as a settlement is going there from New South Wales to cultivate and manufacture flax. But this I fancy will scare some of them. Who would suppose that the Embargo[4] would extend to N.S. Wales and yet it has deprived the Judge Advocate of his Cheshire Cheese. Well it can't be helped. I must wait patiently. I am fearful I shall hardly be able to write to Eliot, Morgan, or Storks by the Experiment. I shall try however. But my fingers are ready to drop off – I have so much writing, my dear fellow. I am hardly got through it. Bligh keeps me constantly employed. I must now go to bed. Pray remember me kindly to Storks and Morgan. God bless him and Morgan, I must not forget my benefactor Reese; I hope he is well Mrs Reese's health quite restored. Are you often there? I am tired out …

Sydney 27 April 1810
My Dearest Mother,

Once more I have the pleasure of addressing you from this remote Corner of the world and assuring you that, though I have had a most laborious and most painful task, to go through since I last wrote my health is thank God much restored. I am gaining strength every day and by the time you receive this letter I have no doubt I shall have been re-established for a considerable time. I wrote to you at great length by the Experiment which sailed the 13th March last under charge of Colonel Foveaux and directed all my letters to the banking House of Messrs Coutts and Co. I at the same time enclosed to you Sydney Gazettes from the period of our arrival to that date. These Gazettes though not interesting in themselves will give you some idea of the Colony and the prices of different articles, and of other things that may be amusing to learn. These different packages I hope reached you in safety. For I should be indeed sorry, on my own account if any accident has happened to them, for I was but very weak when I wrote my letter and it was therefore a work of much time and labour, which I would be mortified to have thrown away. The Reason of my expressing any kind of apprehension is that there has already been a Report, though I believe perfectly without grounds that the Experiment was totally lost between this place and New Zealand. In my letters I stated our present situation, order of life, servants etc etc etc at great length; endeavouring as much as minutely as I could to give you a complete insight into our family arrangements. Only a day after the sailing of the Experiment Captain Brooks arrived in the Simon Cock. The moment of his arrival was to me very tantalizing. For as I was going out the Door to open the Court of Civil Jurisdiction where the other Members were waiting I met Captain Brooks who presented to me a large Packet of letters. Tho' I was beyond anything impatient, I had not time to open them but was obliged to content myself with giving them up to Eliza, and actually I tried twenty causes that morning before I returned home …

29th We yesterday dined at Government House, at a farewell dinner given to Colonel and Mrs Paterson – it was but stupid. Mrs Macquarie has not the art of making people feel happy also comfortable around her. There were in all seventeen persons present. Mr and Mrs M's dinners are much too small as the dinners usually given in the Colony are too profuse. At the top (where Captain Antill, the aide de corp presides) there was a Soup removed by a very small boiled Turkey, at the Bottom (where Captain Cleveland the Brigade Major sits) there was a piece of Roast Beef. The sides were fricassee, curried Duck, Kidneys and Tongue, the corners vegetables; – 2nd Course at the top, Stewed Oysters, bottom wild ducks, sides and corners tartlet, jellies and vegetables in the middle there was an Epergne.[5] The table was very large, and one might have danced a Reel between the dishes. In the evening a Colonial Brig, came into Port, from the Bay of Islands, New Zealand. She brought us the grateful news of the arrival of the Experiment at that place, and that Lt. Col. Foveaux had sailed from thence on the 22nd in a very fine vessel called the Speke. I have no doubt that he will arrive in England very safely with my despatches. You will see in the papers I send you, the shocking account of the loss of the

Boyd, and the massacre of the crew and passengers by Tippackee, one of the Chiefs of New Zealand, and others of the Natives. These accursed cannibals cut their poor unfortunate victims Limb from Limb and eat them before their own faces. Tippackee had been frequently at Sydney and had much attention shewn him while here, except during the time when Colonel Johnston had the Command when he was rather neglected and it has been supposed that he committed this shocking outrage in order to revenge this neglect. The Natives in this country are extremely treacherous and savage and one strong characteristic of them is that where blood is spilt, they will have blood in return: no matter whether innocent or guilty blood. A Captain of a Ship of the name of Luttrell was recently tried before me at a Court of Criminal Jurisdiction for shooting at Tedbury a Native of this Country and wounding him in the face. I held the Court in my own house. Bennellong who is so often mentioned in Collins' narrative was present during the trial. He was acquitted. My garden was full of Blacks and all expected me to hang Luttrell. As that was not the case, in conformity to their own custom, a few days after they speared an unfortunate settler, beyond Parramatta, the Spear went in one side of his body and out at the other, the man has however recovered.

1st May I am so much interrupted I can hardly find time to get on with my letter. Commodore Bligh embarked on Friday last with his daughter Mrs Putland in great form and solemnity. This day Colonel and Mrs Paterson embarked. The Grenadier Company was drawn out to receive him. He is very infirm, and I hardly expect he will survive a Winter Passage around Cape Horn. His character is mild and amiable and even in this country I never heard anyone speak ill of him. Mrs Paterson is a very sensible, good natured and pleasant woman. We have been on very intimate terms with them and have every reason to regret their departure, where they have not left anyone to supply their places. How much did I long for the time of my embarkation and return to be at hand! A year or two, my Dearest Mother will soon pass away, and then nothing shall limit us, but those circumstances which mortals must yield to, from any revisiting our native Country and embracing those we hold so dear. We have lately heard of the death of Colonel Collins, author of the narrative and Lt Governor of the Derwent, in Van Dieman's Land.

He was near 70 years of age, and one of my predecessors in the Office of Judge Advocate. His death was very sudden and it is reported that it was partly occasioned by the distress he experienced on learning that his conduct in regard to Governor Bligh had been disapproved at home. An enormous Bill has been seen up here to the Governor here for the expense of his burial which was publick. It amounted to £500 which is considered a complete job. Colonel Collins is for the present to be succeeded in the command by Captain Murray of the 73rd Regiment. The situation is a pleasant one, because it is a Command and attended with a number of perquisites, opportunities, and comforts, attached to commands. The salary is £450 pr annum. Captain Murray is a married Man and of course his wife accompanies him. This is a still further reduction of our Society here which in regard to ourselves has been reduced by having quarrelled with Mr Carter, the Surgeon of the 73rd Regiment. On my arrival here I continued very unwell for some time. We were then very intimate with Mr and Mrs Carter. The former attended me, but did not understand my case, nor take pains to understand it. Following the entreaties of my Friends, especially Colonel Foveaux and Colonel Paterson, I called in Mr Redfern, by far the cleverest professional man in this Colony, in addition to Mr Carter, at this he was piqued, chose to consider himself affronted and has not spoken since. A very short time after our arrival Mrs Carter was confined. Eliza never missed seeing her two or three times a day, provided her with things which were absolutely quite necessary for her, and not to be purchased here; we promised to stand sponsors for the little boy. Eliza sent it a little frock. Mrs Carter after allowing her boy to wear it a week absolutely sent it back again. The loss of their society is truly small; for Carter is quite uneducated, unconnected and illiterate and consequently conceited, for ignorance and conceit are almost always inseparable companions. The Society now here is very limited indeed; I am not sorry for it, am quite domestic; Eliza even more so; we are never more happy than when we are at home together and I shall now be better able to continue those Plans of Recovery which I at present act upon. I think after, the first expences, I shall be enabled to make the Fees of the situation meet our ordinary expenditure: it is always present to my mind that I came here to save money and not to spend it …

I have been obliged to incur extremely heavy expences indeed. But this I trust, is now over. I have bought almost the whole of my furniture which notwithstanding I have been as frugal as I could be in that respect, has cost me more than £300 – [Eliza expecting second child] I must, and will, notwithstanding your superstitions on that Head, call it Robert – and if he passes as good a Man as his Grandfather, I shall be contented, tho' it be not more fortunate. Though this is not altogether the place you would like, It would give me a pleasure I cannot express to see you here. I could promise you everything clean twice, good Beef and Mutton and my own Eggs, fowls, Ducks, Geese and Turkies. I have now in my Yard a very fine Sow ready to pig, between 50 and 60 Fowls, 8 Geese and two Turkies, but I have a considerable stock of Ducks, Geese and Turkies coming from the Hawkesbury. I feed them with Maize, Wheat (which I have from the stores) cabbages etc etc … Perhaps I might buy them as cheap – as I now get them by feeding them myself but I have the pleasure of having them about me; and what is of more consequence is that I am sure of getting the best kind at a moment's notice, whereas there are many days when a Fowl and a Turkey could not be got in Sydney for love or money. We live very plainly and as little expensively as possible we have a good Cook and when we have a party. I should be not any ashamed if the greatest Epicure were to sit at Table. I assure you Eliza is famous for the Dinners she provides. Our Cook is a Man Cook and makes scraps and made Dishes extremely well. I would you were, my dear Father here to see us … It gave us both much pleasure to hear of the safe arrival of Mr and Mrs G. Knox from Madeira. They behaved with great attention and kindness to Eliza, from which I of course felt much gratification … I hope Mrs G. Knox is perfectly recovered without danger of relapsing. She is a very great favourite of mine and I find they have been speaking in praise of Eliza's singing. She has indeed a sweet voice, of great compass and with a little more practice would modulate it very well. But we have not any Instrument which is a loss we both feel extremely. It would be a source of much amusement to Eliza when I am engaged in business. Mrs Paterson had a small Pianoforte but she asked for it £40 and the sounding board was broken and the instrument was in other respects not a good one. I offered her £26 for it, but it was not accepted, tho it did not cost her more than £25 and she used it for more than 10 years. Pray, my dear Mother, tell Jeffery that I should wish my first spare money should be appropriated to the purchase of a small pianoforte by Broadwood, with Pedals and additional Keys, as good of its Kind as can be. To come safe though it first to be packed in tin, soldered down, and then put in a strong Iron bound, wooden case. Do not be deterred by the Expense of Packing and shipping for the tin will sell here for treble that expense. Broadwood will take upon himself the whole trouble of packing and shipping for he did so with Mrs Macquarie who brought out a charming grand piano, packed in this manner, without sustaining the slightest injury while one of Mrs Couter's packed in a different manner was quite spoiled. If the Piano should be sent, I should like a few Books as well selected Music to be sent with it including Songs, Operas, Sonata's Libretto's etc of Mazzinghi, Von Loch, Hayden, Pleyel and others – at King's Wharf in a transport taken up for the conveyance of stores or Convicts, would I have no doubt bring this to me freight free, more especially, if, as I am Judge of the Admiralty; or the Master of a Private ship might bother for I have a good deal to do with these kinds of Gentlemen …

I return you many thanks, My Dearest Mother, for your kind intentions of sending me a Cheshire Cheese. It certainly would have been acceptable, for in the first place I should have recollected the Giver, in the next articles of that kind are here very scarce, and when cheapest sell for three shillings the Pound. Cheshire Cheese however is extremely apt to decay and rot on the Voyage, on account of their richness, the Cheese that carries best and always continues good is the Pine apple cheeses, Tongues, Hams, and things of that kind, especially English cured ones are very dear and very scarce. It is a very difficult thing to salt meat here, in the hot weather impossible for it will actually breed maggots while on the table before you. But the cold weather has now come and I have sent up to the Hawkesbury for a fat pig to salt it down, as one of my orderly Constables, understands it well, and would do it, for a glass of grog. Brandy is now very dear again, the Officers of the Colony, and among them myself, had delivery of 30 Gallons of Brandy at 13d the gallon which I shall sell shortly for three pounds the Gallon. This is one of the ways of meeting the expences of this expensive place. My Commission as

Judge of the Admiralty Court has not yet arrived. There will be very little business in that department. I endeavour, my Dearest Mother to guide my conduct in my official capacity by the strict principles of rectitude. For the wisdom of my decisions I cannot answer. That they were dictated by impartiality, I am sure. I had to try 251 Causes in the Civil Court. I ordered every one to be regularly entered and numbered in the list, and tried them in the order they were entered in without any respect to rich or poor great or small. Out of 251 causes there were but three appeals, in all of which my decisions were affirmed by the Governor, I wish you could see either Colonel Paterson or Colonel Foveaux, the Account they could give you of me would be ample and I'm sure gratifying to your own feelings. Were you to know all, I have had to do, you would agree with me, that no Young man was ever placed in as ridiculous a situation, and had I been aware of the difficulties I have had to encounter of that total want of System that prevails here, and of the little or no assistance that can be given me here. I should have been afraid to accept the situation. Commodore Bligh, has given me a great deal of trouble, I have had to encounter in him a most eager spirit of Revenge, which to attain its object would have gladly stept over every obstacle interposed by the principles of Justice. But I was determined not to sanction by my name the smallest injustice or illegality. But enough of this.

Partly probably to my differing so much in opinions from the Commodore, He and Mrs Putland did not invite us to any of her dinner parties and thought he could treat me as he did my predecessor. At last Mrs Putland sent an invitation to a Ball and Supper she gave, which we declined. This caused some little surprise. The Lt Governor, one day, asked me the reason and I told him that I did not conceive that the Commodore had paid me that attention and respect which my official situation and personal character demanded and therefore I declined going to his Ball.

I have no dislike to the Governor and shall always be ready to do my duty towards him, and towards the public in the ablest manner I can. Captain Brooks brought me many letters from my friends and a letter of recommendation from Mr P. Kinnon. I was not able to pay any attention to him at first on account of the continued sitting of the Civil Court; but he has since dined here and I shall now have more licence to attend to him … His ship the Simon Cock has already returned and I regret I did not write by it very late in the evening and yet I wish to complete this letter. I feel that I am pleasing you, and that delights me so much that I cannot cease writing for then I must cease to please …

Sydney NSW 2 May 1810
My Dearest Jeffery,

I wrote you full accounts of our safe arrival at this place at the close of last year. I sent with other letters under charge of Lt Col Foveaux by the Experiment.

I was somewhat disappointed in not receiving my Commission as Judge of the Vice Admiralty Court here, either by the Ann or by the Simon Cock, for which I was extremely anxious. The next Store Ship, a convict ship will bring it out. I am not anxious for it, on account of the Salary which I will expect be merely nominal, but on account of the additional respect it may procure me. The continued sitting of the Civil Court and the fatigue and trouble it caused me, prevented me from paying much attention to Captain Brooks, but I have since asked him to dinner and now at leisure to take notice of him. I must not forget to acknowledge the receipt of newspapers of different kinds down to 8 September inclusive and also of Monthly Magazines and an Edinburgh Review to which I should wish to be added either the monthly or annual Review …

I think I mentioned in my last letter to Storks that I had been presiding in a Court of Criminal Jurisdiction. The Court sat every day for a week excepting one day and also excepting Sunday. There were twelve prisoners tried: two were sentenced to death. It may appear strange but I did not feel myself agitated in the least at the opening of the Court. But went through the business with a coolness surprising myself and with very great ease. I sat in my Silk Gown and Wig and pronounced the sentence of death with my Cap on. I must say the Prisoners took it as coolly as I did for notwithstanding I find in the papers that my Brother Bayley when pronouncing the sentence of the law burst into tears and was obliged to turn his head aside. The Devil a tear, could Mr Justice Bent squeeze out. This has proved to me an observation I have often felt on these occasions; that it is much more easy for a Judge to cry, when he has on his left hand a fine smart fellow, with a Silk Coat, Bayley's second, and white Wand, on his right a Jury Box, a good many big wigs, below him, and a crowd of ladies above him, a fine court to sit in and a good salary; than it is for me who was obliged to sit out in a bit of a Hovel with no one to remark how extremely agitated I am, no High Sheriff etc etc. Give me all the above appendages and as good a Salary and I will cry with ease a Judge on the Bench. But Good God if you were to see my Dear Fellow, the Court I sit in and the Crowd I am surrounded by you would split yourself with laughing. The two Prisoners were pardoned by the Governor on certain conditions which they have already broken. Notwithstanding all things I conducted everything with as much form and regularity as I could: examined all the Witnesses and took down all the evidence with my own hands which not a little fatigued me. I also prepared all the Indictments and entered the plea and Judgement of the Court in a regular manner. The Court usually met at 10 o'clock and adjourned at three o'clock. The Criminal Court gives much less trouble than the Civil Court and also much less difficulty.

3rd May. We yesterday dined at a large party given by Col. O'Connell and the Officers of the 73rd Regt. We dined in the Lt. Governors House, where there is a room much larger than any in the colony – I should think we were altogether, as many of 40 persons. The Governor and Mrs Macquarie were there, Commodore Bligh and Mrs Putland, his daughter. Captain and Mrs Dawes etc etc. We had a very good dinner, and soon after part of us adjourned to Government House to tea and Conds. From what Cause, I can hardly say, partly I think from my feeling myself obliged to give Opinions on points submitted to me by him and the Governor, very different from those which the Commodore wished me to give, partly from certain advice I have given to the Governor, definitely resulting from some neglect on the part of him I have not received that attention from the Commodore which was my due. He has not invited us to any of his Dinner Parties. This I felt with proper spirit and let the Governor know that I did. Some time since Mrs Putland gave a Ball and a Supper, to which we among the rest were invited. But we declined going, this mortified him exceedingly. The Lt. Governor mentioned the circumstance afterwards, and said how sorry the Commodore was that we absented ourselves. I supplied that Commodore Bligh had not shewn me that attention and respect which my Official situation and personal Character demanded and that I could not think of visiting him until he chose to explain the reason of it. Yesterday the Lt Governor (who is really an excellent Fellow, and with whom I am very intimate) told me he mentioned to the Commodore what I had said – that he was concerned at it, and that he did not mean or intend any want of respect, but that his not having invited us proceeded from an idea that if the prosecution of different persons in the colony were carried on and the Commodore, who would be the prosecutor and myself (who would be the Judge) were much together the publick might make unfavourable observations upon it, and the Parties prosecuted might think it hard that the Commodore should monopolize all the professional assistance in the Colony. I shall of course admit the apology tho' I know it to be unfounded. For in the first place, the mere invitation to a formal party could not have produced that effect; and in the next place Bligh is not a Man of those refined and delicate Sentiments very far otherwise indeed – who to have obtained the end of punishing with severity some persons in the Colony would have adopted any means in his power and notwithstanding publick observation would have officially called upon me for every assistance that I could afford. O'Connell added that Mrs Putland wished to be intimate with Eliza, and to court her acquaintance I said that could not be as Mrs P. was about to leave the Colony in three days. But, says the Colonel, suppose she should stay behind; I immediately divined the fact and now know that the Colonel is going to marry Mrs Putland! who has prepared all her accommodation on board the Hindostan, embarked her luggage and herself and with her Father taken leave of the Governor with the usual formalities. I must give you some account of her. She is about 28, very small, a nice little figure – and rather a sensible face. Dresses with *some taste, very thinly, and compensates for the want of petticoats wears breeches, or rather trousers. She is conceited and affected to a greater degree than any woman I ever saw before; Everything is studied about her – her walk – her talking – everything – and you have but to observe the mode of her sitting down and this part of her character you would see at once. I am told that she is extremely violent and passionate; so much so and then to fling a plate or a candlestick at her Father's Head. But on account of party spirit in this place, I speak this 'cum grano salis'[with a grain of salt]. She is very clever, and accomplished and plays remarkably well on the piano forte. After her arrival in this country with her father, she married a Mr Putland, a Lieut. in the navy and I am informed a very nice young Man. It is also said that both Bligh and herself treated him like a Pig or a Dog. Putland died about three days before Bligh's arrest, and she is reported left his widow £300 pr annum – which was then reduced to £100 per annum if she married again. She is very fond of being among the first, wherever she is, and rather than go back as a private Individual, remains here as Lieut. Governors wife. O'Connell I think, a liberal, goodhearted, generous Man – open, brave, extravagant. But he is not handsome, he is not of a good constitution, having seen much service, and is, I should think 45. He was educated in France, born in Ireland, and has been in the French Service. I fear he has nothing but his pay, and he is very expressive and extravagant. I lament extremely this marriage in the first place, I dislike her, In the next place, it crushes the hopes I had formed of seeing complete harmony restored in the Colony and encourages at once that party spirit, which renders this place more unpleasant than you can imagine. During Mrs Putland's continuance here, there must be two parties in the Colony. I have many other reasons also which it would be tedious to develop. Colonel O'Connell is to be with me this morning after breakfast (you see I am an early riser) to talk to me in private and as I suppose settle the Marriage Articles.*

After this long episode, you must here permit me to give you some account of the proceedings in the civil Court. From the want of proper Agents and Attornies, a very great deal of trouble is thrown upon me – in order to procure regularity and to know the real amount of business before the court, I ordered that every cause should be regularly entered with my Clerk, and that they should be tried in the order in which they were entered, that is the entry should close on a certain day. But from the Ignorance of the parties this was not so much attended to as it ought to have been, and I was obliged to keep the entry open for a much longer time than I had intended. In all there were 251 cases entered, but it was what we call in England a very rotten paper: for most of the causes were undefended. There are no pleadings whatever, for the patent directs that all pleas etc shall be tried in a summary manner. In cases under £10 the writ is merely a Summons to appear and defend the action. But upon an affidavit of debt above £10 the defendant is held to this by the Provost Marshall who executes all the praecipes of the Courts here. Upon the appearance of the Plaintiff and Defendant, the Case is heard, and the Defendant pleads viva voce. This is most embarrassing mode of proceeding – for the Parties wander from the Point so much. The Plaintiff endeavouring to introduce as many different grounds of action as he can, and the defendant as many different grounds of defence. I now see more than the utility of official Pleadings and wish it could be established here. The Court consisted of myself and Mr Riley and a Mr Palmer; on our first meeting; The Governor's precept for assembling the Court is read, and the members sworn: then the business begins. I have endeavoured as much as possible to make the practice here conform to that in England, but as there is no profession of the Law here, the Rules I establish are not generally taken notice of; some know them, others do not, and where every man is obliged to be his own Lawyer, you know he has a Fool for his Client. You cannot form an idea of the illegality and irregularities that have prevailed here, and it would exceed the bounds of a letter were I to attempt describing them. There were some serious actions tried before me which originated in the late disturbances in this colony, which gave me much trouble and anxiety. The first was an action brought by a Mr Hook here against Colonel Paterson and several others for a false imprisonment in which he laid his damages at £10,000. The action was brought under the following circumstances, which occurred subsequent to the arrest of Governor Bligh and which Lt Gov Paterson had the command. Bligh wrote a Proclamation declaring the New South Wales Government to be illegal, the 102nd Regiment in a state of mutiny and diverse persons to be Rebels, this paper was distributed by Hook which being known he was brought before a Bench of Magistrates and by them held to Bail, to appear before a Criminal Court to answer a Charge exhibited against him for circulating papers tending to disturb the peace of the Colony. He gave Bail. A short time after a Criminal Court was assembled by virtue of a Precept from Lt Governor Paterson. Hook appeared before it and an Information was exhibited against him, to which he refused to plead, denying the legality of the court upon which the court took the indictment pro contemps [for the present] and sentenced him to pay a fine of £50 and be imprisoned one Month. The Court under my direction, found the Defendants Not Guilty, from which Hook appealed to the Governor who confirmed my Verdict. And Hook has now lodged an appeal to the King in Council. On this account I enclose to you the reasons in which a verdict was founded. This was an extremely important Cause, and I know I have taken a great responsibility upon myself but I think the decision was right. If Hook had obtained a verdict, there would have been no end to the actions, brought for circumstances which occurred during the late Revolution. This consideration, however, did not influence me in the least, tho' I saw it and soon after my arrival advised the Governor, to publish a general act of Indemnity; but he did not like to take that upon himself – tho' he is now sorry he did not do it. If the above appeal comes in I should wish you to attend and report it to me. The next case was an action of false Imprisonment brought by G. Crossley the cidevant Attorney, convicted of perjury against Johnston and other members of a Criminal Court, by which he was transported for 7 years, confined for two years and released by the present Governor. The Court was illegally constituted but I directed a verdict for the Plaintiff, Damages £500 because the proceedings were totally opposite to the Common Principles of Justice. I shall endeavour to send you a copy of the Minutes. There was an appeal to the Governor, who confirmed the Verdict, but from a compassionate Feeling reduced the damages to £300 which have been paid and accepted. I am certain that all parties in the above cases were satisfied that my decision was directed by a wish to do Complete Justice. I am sure I felt no bias – for I neither knew nor cared for any of the parties. Some other actions were also tried rather Interesting, but I have not time to address to them. I have lately a great deal of business to get through, which harasses and fatigues me extremely. The number of complaints that are daily made to me are astonishing and the complainants all expect immediate Redress. In England, if a person finds himself injured he applies to his Attorney and the Expense attending these applications have this good effect, that it obliges persons to look over little trifling injuries and put up with them as part of the Rubs a person must meet with in this world. But here as Law is not attended with any expence, or at most a very trifling one, I am tormented with Complaints of the most ridiculous nature. I must give you a Sample of one. A Woman came to me when I was very busy and sent in for me. I desired her to call another time. But as she said her complaint was of a most particular nature, I at last consented to hear it there and then; Upon which she said 'My Lord, I sent my little Girl to John Collis for a pint of Beer. She goes and John gives me only half a pint, and takes all the money. Upon that I goes to John myself and I says, Johnny How is it you have sent me only half a pint of Beer, and taken all my money. Upon which John says, Ax my A-E, and it is very hard My Lord etc etc etc. And this is the way, I am teased all day.

So much for the nature of the business – now I shall say a word or two about the Emoluments about which I have no doubt you will be anxious to hear. The amount of Fees I have received in the last four months is £142.18.5½ – but I suppose that I have from £20 to £30 due to me, which my Clerk has not collected. I think I may fix the yearly amount with safety at £600 pr annum. In this Account I have included fees of all descriptions, publick and private and I have drawn several conveyances, Wills etc etc. For entering each cause I have 5d and the same for each Verdict. I have not yet sold my Cape Wine for the last importation of Brandy has considerably reduced its price, but I will engage that in less than six weeks I shall sell it for £100. You will be surprised to find that we have been obliged to be parted with Elizabeth. She was really too bad for anything. Her Insolence, extravagances, and Ingratitude were intolerable. The Colonel was here yesterday morning as I mentioned. It is very true that he is going to marry Mrs Putland, and it is, I may say to the universal sorrow of the whole colony. I was incorrect in some of the Facts relative to Mrs P. above mentioned. She was married in England. Her fortune is £200 pr annum and by the will of her late husband, she has all his personal property – and had a rent charge of £200 pr annum and in the *event of the death of his Mother £100 pr annum more, so long as she continues unmarried. She has a farm here of 600 acres and some cattle and the Governor has made a grant to O'Connell of 3000 acres of land in whatever part of the Colony he pleases. This is to be settled upon her and I am to draw the marriage settlements. The more's the Pity, for I hate having anything to do with such an accursed match …*

We are still in the same house as the alterations on our Official House haven't yet been begun; nor do I know when they will begin, but we are very comfortable in the house we now occupy, and very little anxious to remove from it. Remember me kindly to Bright – tell him that from my Situation, I shall be able to send him some valuable seeds, and to send him them gratis. But they are enormously dear; and I have not yet been able to set about procuring them. I have been very ill but am now better… I did not expect that my Uncle would ever get much by going to Law; he was too fearful of expence. In all litigations and disputes it is always the surest and cheapest plan to submit a clear statement of facts to an Eminent Lawyer to take his advice, and when once you have determined to go to law, go through it without flinching … I have been very much taken in by bringing Bank's Nephew with me as a Clerk. He is not fit for it. His education has not been good enough and he is extremely ignorant, without possessing any strong desire to acquire knowledge. He may be useful as a Copying Clerk but at present from his want of attention to spelling and total Ignorance of the nature of things he has to copy he is extremely incorrect. I ought to have brought out a person that had been educated in an Attorney's Office. I could have made it very well worth the attention of a person of that description. For at the lowest the salary and Fees would amount to £200 pr annum and in addition I could have got him rations, house, and a servant, free of Expense. I have now in my office an Attorney, who came out a Convict for Forgery. He is very clever, understands conveyancing etc etc But is confoundedly addicted to drinking. I allow him to take the greater part of the Clerk's Fees as his compensation. There is no place here worth your consideration, I am certain. If Ministers would create two offices of King's Advocate, and Attorney General and unite them in your person with a good salary – and also send out a regular 'Corps Judicial' it would then be worth your while to come out: for a pretty sum might be made here by private practice. But it never would do to come out without a Government appointment. For in this place unless a Man is connected with the Government He is Nobody. I have a famous Cook, and if I should see you here I'll engage to furnish you with much more substantial Chops, than the Chinese Chop. Pray, My Dear Jeffery say everything that is kind and affectionate to my Dear Friends, Stocks, Eliot and Ingram, I ought to have written to them all – and I fear they will think me unkind in having omitted to do it. But assure them it is not my fault … To Mrs Reese I must be particularly remembered – she ranks with my most valued Friends – and I trust her Health is quite restored. I am most sorry to find that Morgan has been ill, but in this I trust he has been restored. His Friend Mr Birch, Paymaster 73rd Regt is again in a most deplorable state of illness and quite deranged. His wife who has lately been confined, is truly afflicted. Tell Robert Stocks, to whom let all the family I desire remembrances, that P– continues a common sailor and behaves as all other common sailors, there are no hopes of his Reformation – Adieu my Dearest Jeffery.

Sydney July 27 1810
My Dearest Mother

I wrote to you at considerable length, as well to my dear Father, Brother, and several of my friends by H.M.S. Hindostan, which with the Dromedary and Porpoise, left this Harbour some time in May last. I hope those letters will come to hand, long before I say any thing further, I cannot help expressing our sorrow and disappointment at the arrival of the Concord, in this part, direct from England which she left in January last without bringing a single letter from any of our Friends, I am sure however upon reflection, that she must have left without your knowledge and I understand that from the jealousy which prevails among the traders to this colony, it is but too much the custom to slip away with as much secrecy as possible. Though the Concord brought us no news, I am determined that she shall be the means of carrying you some. She leaves this place on Sunday, for Rio Janeiro, from which her letters will be forwarded to

England and I cannot but hope embrace with eagerness the opportunity it affords us of giving you further intelligence concerning those who are so happy to receive so large a proportion of your affections. But I fear the shortness of my time and the number of letters here to write, will not permit me to enter into details as long as I could wish. Since our arrival here my unfortunate illness, and the confusion in which I found my office and the business I had to go through, has prevented me from keeping a Journal which was at first my intention. These obstacles are now in a great measure removed, and I shall in future endeavour to keep a regular one for your satisfaction and amusement ... now, thank God, I am as healthy as I ever was, and able to attend all my avocations without feeling the smallest fatigue ... We are still occupying the same house but shall not continue in the possession of it very long – I have little doubt that in about 12 months time we shall be inhabiting our own new Mansion which is already begun upon some time, the Governor offered to contract with any person to build an appropriate house for me. But no satisfactory proposals were received. Happening one day to say casually to the Governor that I would myself build the house, if the Government would advance me a proper sum of money; the Governor said he should be very glad to do so. Accordingly as agreement was made between us, that I should build a House and offices to my own liking, and that I should receive for that purpose the sum of £300 sterling and 1000 gallons of spirits. I have contracted with a person to build the House and Offices and finish them in every respect, fit for occupation except glazing for £1950. The Spirits are not yet in the colony but he has agreed to take the 1000 gallons at 35d per gallon, which makes £1750 and £200 in Colonial Money which is at a discount of 20%, so that I shall have £160 left for Glazing the House and other purposes. Besides this Governor says he shall take care I do not sustain any loss. The House will I am sure be superior to any in the Colony and I hope you will receive safely with this letter three plans of it, one of the front, one of the back, the other of the Ground Plan and Offices. The whole of the present Garden will be a lawn in front of the house, and the Governor is to give me a Kitchen Garden elsewhere. The Centre part is to contain three storeys, and on the Ground floor there will be a dining Room, 26 feet by 16 a Drawing Room of the same dimensions, and a study 16 by 13 – the entrance will be at the back – in the back of the House offices will form three sides of a square ...

*I hope you will think the plan unites a good deal of convenience with some
taste. The house is to be plastered in imitation of stone and the corners to
have rustick covers of stone.*

*I have lately been doing a great number of things for the Governor
for which he has expressed himself greatly obliged to me. But I cannot
bring myself to ask favours and flatter as some people do. There are
several, who I dare say have more influence at Government House than
I have ... but I am proud to say that there are none who have rendered
him such assistance as much as myself. I have at his request drawn up a
plan for establishing a new Police, drawn up regulations to new model
the market, offered to manage all the colonial laws and Regulations in
one Code and not withstanding my illness have never missed attending
the regular meetings of the magistrate since I came into the colony.
Some time ago, he expressed his intention of giving me a grant of land,
and desired me to choose in what part of the country I would have it.
I am taking an excursion up the country for that purpose. I fixed upon
some ground by the beautiful River Nepean, on one side; through the
middle of which a creek runs. On my return he told me he should give
me 1200 acres, some Cows, sheep and some stockmen, to take care
of my cattle. The cows and sheep are to be paid for in kind from their
increase. I am very well pleased with this, and am going to call the
estate Moulsey and the little creek the Mole. The land is fine, beautifully
varied by the near hills and vallies, which are green even this time of
the year. It is about 40 Miles from Sydney and its native name is Byaloe.
It is very fine grazing land and will not require any expence. I mean
to have a Man there, who will live in a bark hut of his own building
who besides, being victualled by the Government expense will receive a
yearly remuneration from me. He will take care of the cattle, which will
range about and feed on the finest pasturage and will have nothing to
do but increase and multiply. Every calf is from £10 to £15, the moment
it is dropped. The grazing farmer is the only really wealthy person in
this colony. The Profit is certain. The expense and risk nothing. It is in
this way the McArthurs, Marsdens, and Wentworths have become rich.
I went upon the excursion to which I have just alluded on Saturday
last, in company with Mr Hinch, Paymaster of the 73rd and Mr Bayley*

formerly of the 102nd a son of Colonel Bayley, and near relation of the Earl of Lexbridge. We performed our Journey on horseback and slept the first night at Parramatta about 16 miles from Sydney. Parramatta is a pretty but a straggling kind of village; the Road has nothing remarkable in it, but its badness and its novelty in passing through a forest of heavy trees. The next day we stopt at Mr Bayley's farm about 14 miles further on. The road leads entirely through the woods which are not however very thick, and presents occasionally some very pleasing views. Mr Bayley has about 1400 acres, about 40 of which are cleared. He has about 1000 very fine sheep as any in the Colony and the buildings on the farm are very neat and clean. The next day we rode about 10 miles further to look at some ground, he recommended me to take. We did not go quite so far as the Nepean River – but I saw enough to determine to choose my land there. The trees are not too close, nor too large, so that there will be but little trouble in clearing the ground, which appears very good especially for pasturage. It abounds in Kangaroos, and on our return we had a very fine chase after a female one, which the dogs killed in about ten minutes. It weighed 40lb. The Kangaroo makes astonishing leaps, sometimes, nay frequently when pressed it will leap 40 to 50 feet at one jump. The common people here are very fond of the flesh, and the skin makes very tolerable leather. We retired to a 5 o'clock dinner at the Bayleys farm and at night or rather at 2 o'clock next morning, as the Moon rose we all mounted our horses, and Mr Birch and myself rode to Sydney, without stopping, and arrived about 8 in the morning. I was fearful the Concord would sail out without giving me sufficient time to write my letters. Thus we rode nearly 60 miles through the roads in 24 hours and this is a sufficient proof, I think, of my good health, more especially as I have not suffered in the least from it. I have no particular news to tell you of in this place – it is as dull as ever. Lately however a Race Course has been established here, under the sanction of the Governor which by and by may tend to enliven the scene a little. Every thing here continues almost as dear as it used to be. All kinds of Butcher's meat are retailing at 1s 6d per lb. But lately I have bought a whole pig at a time at one shilling per lb dead. Beef I have from the Stores, so that Mutton is the only meat one has to buy at that price. I intend if possible to send you by the first secure opportunity, some of the living curiosities of this Country. I have now two blue mountains parrots – two Rose Hill parrots, a lone King Parrot – and two New Zealand mocking birds. The latter are singularly beautiful and extraordinary and they are wonderfully brilliant in their plumage, nothing can be more splendid than the appearance of the woods on a sunshiny day, from the immense variety of parrots of all description and sizes which are constantly flying from bough to bough, and the number of elegant and fragrant shrubs. Indeed in Birds and Shrubs this colony may vie with if not surpass any country in the known world. From some time past the weather has been extremely fine. It is now the depth of Winter, and we have fires all the day through altho' at noon, the Sun has considerable power. At this time of year, the Climate is truly charming. We have an abundance of vegetables in the Garden. Sallad, cabbage, broccoli, beans and peas in great perfection. This Day is Sunday and Eliza and myself had two favourite dishes and yours, my Dear Mother, for our dinner. A small piece of boiled Pork, of our own salting and some nice young beans from our own garden.

Sydney 30 July 1810
My Dear Jeffery

… I have never felt myself better in health than I am now at this moment and enjoy it all the more from the remembrance I have of my severe indisposition. Our situation here is precisely the same in most respects as when we wrote last. The same dullness, the same uniformity and the same dearness of all articles still remain. The Mare from which Eliza had her fall, is, I think for her size, the best in the Colony. I gave Captain Piper £90 for her but have since sold her to the paymaster of the 73rd for £115. – down – so that I lose nothing by that. I gave sometime back 30 gallons of spirits £50 of some Cape Wine for a young Gelding: that I have since changed for a very nice horse for Eliza. I have in the room of the other got an excellent mare for myself, and am now I think, very well off in regard to horses, without which it is here impossible to have amusement or exercise.

[Recounts trip to Nepean and how he will raise cattle] when, fat and return them into the Government store. – This is the mode that is adopted here. Mrs Mc Arthur has only three men to take care of her herds of horned cattle and without any other expence returns the fat males into the Government store at 9d per lb. and I know for this she received during the last Quarter Bills on the treasury for £1400. She has very large flocks of sheep and sells every pound of her mutton for sixteen pence. Her profits are amazing. There is no land near Sydney at all worth having. The native name of the place [of the grant] is Byaloe. This may perhaps give it an interest it does not now possess. I own that at present I care but little about it – and only hope that it may be the means of putting something into my pocket. The Changes in the Ministry and the Duel between Lord Castlereagh and Mr Canning have much astonished us. It can not surely be a lasting administration though Lord Wellesly be in. I am surprised to find Sutton Judge Advocate General. How Lucky! And yet people frequently say connections are nothing in the law. By the next Ship, I expect to receive my commission as Judge of the Admiralty and hope there is some emolument attached to it. There has lately been a Vice Admiralty Court held here of which I acted as Judge, by a Commission from the Governor. It was an application from Lord, to remove Mr Wilkinson from being Master of a Vessel called the Star, of which Plummers are registered owners. As the Master opposed it and I thought upon good grounds I dismissed the application. Mr Lord has appealed. Pray send me out Tables of Fees both in the Instance and Prize Courts of the Vice Admiralty: for in the late court from the want of knowing what fees were proper to take I did not take any. A Proctor's Billing costs would be the best guide in many instances.

I have no doubt that Storks continue to be successful in the profession, and to advance by slow but sure degrees. Long may his luck continue. How are all the family and especially Mr and Mrs Reese? I trust you visit familiarly there. He is an excellent young man, and she the best creature in the world. Pray give my best regards to them both. I have several very beautiful birds as soon as I can find a person to trust them to, I shall certainly send some there. I have not forgotten Bright's seeds, but this is not the season to get them. I am afraid they will come dear, everything is so in this Country but I will go the cheapest ways to work. Remember me most kindly to Eliot. I suppose he goes on as usual. How I envy him! His house, his retirement occasionally! After all there is no life like that of a person with a good living. Is Charles Morgan quite well? Has he not been ill at Ramsgate. I think Eliot says so in his letter to me. If he went to Ramsgate to get money, I am afraid he will find it as bad a speculation as to come here for it. Pray remember me most affectionately to him, and scold him for not having written me one letter. – Remember me to John Wild, ah my old friends, John Williams, Courtenay, Bright etc etc and be sure to give me intelligence of the Cumberland sessions. It was my intention to have written to Ireland this opportunity but I must put it off ...

Pray remember me kindly to my Uncle Hart and my dearest Aunt Lyddal, my head is quite puzzled. I continue to send for your united entertainment the Sydney Gazettes, and also the Derwent Gazettes, they may arrive. You observe great improvements have taken place in the town – one of the streets (that where the Judge Advocate's Residence is situated) is called Bent Street.

Sydney 25 October 1810
My Dearest Mother,

...[the arrival of the Canada] You cannot conceive the emotion the arrival of a ship occasions, in this out of the way place, especially when the Signal is made that she comes from England, emotions of disappointment on not receiving letters, of Joy when we are so fortunate as to receive letters from our friends ... I am but just relieved from my long and fatiguing labours which have quite jaded me. The sitting of the Civil Court commenced on August last, and has not been closed for more than a week. There were 445 cases entered for trial, some of a very intricate nature, and of much importance, I had to sit every day and to write of course a great deal. However I went through them all and there

are not 5 appeals from my decisions. But the Governor on hearing, has confirmed my Judgement in all of them. Scarcely was this labour over, when a Criminal Court assembled. The proceedings of this Court closed only yesterday. Add to all this extraordinary business, the meeting of a Bench of Magistrates every Saturday, which has the sitting of a great deal of business and even as ill I have never once omitted to preside at those meetings, since my arrival in this Colony. It would have been a great relief to me had the sailing of the Atalanta been delayed by a week. But as that cannot be. I must again buckle to. The shortness of the time and the stiffness of my Fingers must be my apology, if I fail to write to all those who have so much right to hear from me. Though I was delighted with the effort it must have cost, I cannot express my astonishment that you were determined upon, and that you and my Father had actually completed a journey to Ireland ... I looked upon such an undertaking to have been amongst the number of things impossible. It gave me, however, sincere pleasure to hear the intelligence. It was a thing I had much at heart, as I am convinced any alteration of the scene, but especially such an alteration as would afford you a sight of Hannah and your grandchildren must be attended with high beneficial effects to you and my father. I can confidently express an opinion that this Journey will be remembered with pleasure during the rest of your lives, notwithstanding a thought of that grim visaged, remorseless Irish Taxgatherer may now and then intrude. Thank God! We have no such vermin here. Thieves, rascals, vagabonds what are they to a Tax Gatherer? I'm very happy to hear that Lord Northland is quite well, and am much gratified and obliged to him for his kind expressions of regard and interest for me. Considering the labour and responsibility of the situation and more especially the enormous prices of the necessaries of life here of every description the salary is but small. I am sure you will agree with me that where Meat is 1s 6d per pound, butter 5s Milk 1s per quart tea 2 and three Guineas a pound and the commonest cantwill Muslin 10 shillings per yard, the most rigid reasoning is required to support a family in any degree of decency. A loaf of Bread such as in London would [cost] 1s 2d at most, is now not to be procured, or if procured would cost 4s 5d and yet in this country, among all classes of people, the greatest and most unfounded extravagance prevails. The lowest, even those who can neither read nor write, issue their promissory notes to an astonishing amount which for a time pass current and when presented to the drawer are refused, not with humility or sorrow, but with the most depraved insolence. There is no such thing as Commissariat Credit or necessitated principle or honour: a Merchant here cares no more about having his bills protested or dishonoured than he would about the most trivial occurrence of the day: but immediately sets about drawing others, which he knows must experience the same fate to gull some poor fool or other with. I assure you I would not take the Bill upon London of any Merchant house in this city for 200 for 50 per cent premium – a poorer more unprincipled more extravagant set are not to be mentioned.

F.W who was formerly on the Port au Prince is quite a fine Gentleman has his running horses, his livery servants etc etc. Since his last arrival he has issued, it is said, more than £2000 of his own notes, and has spent in horses as much if not more than £700.

… Our situation and residence is just the same as when I wrote you last. Our house is extremely comfortable, large enough for our wants, and we enjoy in it as much comfort and happiness as we can have in this place. Society is here very limited and by no means choice and that little is very distracted by party spirit and little Jealousies. We are upon a very intimate and pleasant footing at Government house. The Governor is a very good man, always uniformly polite, affable and obliging, and I really believe wishes to make me as comfortable as he can. We went up with them to Parramatta, a few weeks ago, and passed some very pleasant days at Government house. About the first of November he goes upon his tour thro' the Country: if able I shall go with him a part of the way – to settle about my farm etc... I shall have my farm in about a month … He has also given me a lease (at a pepper corn rent) of Garden Island a very fertile little Island at the entrance of Sydney Cove capable of maintaining cows and sheep to supply my table and of producing all kinds of garden vegetables. Mr Curvers Island in Windermere lake is nothing to it either in size or beauty. The Offices of my new House are nearly finished – and I trust that my House itself will be covered in long before you receive this letter. A Supply of Spirits has come in lately which

will enable me to go on very rapidly with it. I had the pleasure of sending you the plan and views of it by the Concord which was bound for Rio. It will be very comfortable when finished the prettiest thing in the colony. Last week Sydney exhibited a gayer scene, than it has ever done since its foundation. Annual races have been established under the Patronage of the Governor, which occurred for the first time on the 15th of October. The Race Course is a piece of Waste Ground on the outskirts of town and called Hyde Park. The course is circular and is exactly one mile and 40 yards round. There are a certain number of subscribers to the Race Course, at whose expense the course was finished and who gave 50 Guineas for a plate to be run for by the subscribers' horses, which was run for on the first day and won by a horse called Chace, belonging to Captain Richie of the 73rd Regiment. The Ladies established 50 Guineas for a Silver Cup which was won by the same horse on the Wednesday and on the Friday a purse of 50 guineas given by the Magistrates was run for and won by a Horse of the name of Scratch. On the Race days, there was an ordinary[6] provided, and in the course of the Week there were two Balls – all passed off extremely well; and both races and balls afforded much amusement.

Ellis ... names almost everything and begins to join little sentences together. Everybody is pleased with him and he is a great favourite at Government house. He is amusing and entertaining beyond description, and I have no doubt, if he lives, he will be very clever. I wish you could see him. He almost always calls me Father Bent, which is my old college nickname ... I have not yet been able to commence a Journal, or copy an account of my stay at the Cape. The confused state of my office is beyond belief. I have everything to do myself – nobody to assist me – and everybody to teach ...I am sorry to hear that my dear Father grieves so much at my absence, let him assure himself that my situation is very comfortable God bless you My dearest Mother May your future years, be years of happiness

Sydney New South Wales 28 February 1811
My Dearest Jeffery,

I take this opportunity afforded by the departure of the Indian Captain Arthur Barclay, for India, of once more writing to you and giving you such information respecting ourselves as may be interesting. As I think it highly probable that we shall have some Vessel sailing directly from this Port to England, I shall defer till then writing to my dear Father and Mother, and any other Friends at home, to all of whom I wrote to very fully by the Atalanta, and to most of whom the contents of this letter will probably be communicated. The Ship Indian arrived here with male Convicts on the 16th December last and brought a small supply of such things as were most wanted here. But unfortunately, she did not bring one single letter from my Family nor any Intelligence whatsoever concerning them or any other of my Friends. I did not feel the disappointment then so much as I do now; for on the very morning she arrived in Sydney Cove Eliza presented me with a sweet little Boy, who, I think, will prove prettier than Ellis, and I hope as clever and good. The little one made its entrance into this troublesome world a few minutes before 5 o'clock on Thursday morning the 16th December 1810, Eliza is now perfectly well recovered and the stranger is improving every hour. We have since made a Christian of him, by the title of Robert Lawrence Bent, after my dear Father – to whom I hope this token of our remembrance and affection will not be unpleasing – and my friend Eliot.

This Place requires one to have Eyes all over and to keep all of them open. Servants are such devils that one is exposed to perpetual depredations, which hurt more by their constant recurrence than by their separate magnitude.

... Birch and myself have bought a Flock of 340 breeding Ewes, six Rams 100 Head of horned Cattle and a Brood Mare. Birch being the Paymaster of the 73rd Regiment advanced the greater part of the money, the Horned cattle come to £1375 and the sheep to £1035.[7] The expense of keeping these is the expense of an Overseer, a Shepherd and a Cowherd, a common hut and two stock yards. The Profits are immense

the Risk nothing. The Cattle have encreased since we had them and both Cows and sheep are as fine as any in the Colony. The horned cattle are considered as the very best bargain that has been made in the colony. I believe I have already told you that Grazing is the most certain mode here of making a Fortune, the profits are so uniform, the expence so trifling in comparison and so early ascertained. There is no trouble and expence incurred in feeding the cattle they have boundless pasturage to range, which is never exhausted; and even at this moment when the Community has suffered severest drought ever known here, the Cattle are as fine and fat as possible. In November I shall sell about 170 lambs at the common price 30 shillings a head, and put 5 Bullocks into the Government Store, which will average at 8p per lb (which is the Government price) at about £24 per head at least. I enclose you a modest Calculation, drawn up by a very sensible man, Mr Broughton, Acting Commissary, which will explain the profits of horned cattle to you. We have an excellent steady old Overseer, a Shepherd and cowherd both very good and both victualled and clothed by Government. I do not mean to Cultivate a single acre of ground, that is a certain and great expense and a very uncertain and small profit. My farm is 43 miles from Sydney at most. I have driven all the way there in a Gig. We have a comfortable weather boarded Hut now up, about 200 Yards from the Nepean and a good Stock yard and sheep yard existing. The River Nepean is the Western boundary of my farm and is a most romantic stream. – Birch's farm 500 acres adjoins mine

My Situation is one of continual difficulty. No regular laws, no judicial body, no settled forms, no regular practitioners. The whole plan too is so radically bad, as to admit of no amendment. Till I had the experience of my present situation I never was sufficiently aware of the absolute necessity of established forms for the due obtainment or execution of Justice. You may reply, But why do you not establish these forms and stick to them – I answer who is to take notice of them. There are here, no regular Attorneys, no Council whose duty it is to make themselves acquainted and to obey those Rules. And where is the use of inventing forms for a parcel of ignorant and uneducated Settlers, who have neither ability nor interest to take notice of these, until they have a Law Suit, the greater part of them can neither read or write.

I merely wish it to be understood that the total want of established forms and a regular judicial body prevents me from observing that uniformity of Conduct, at which is the essence of Justice and subjects me to inconceivable vexation and trouble. If you should, fill a similar situation you would then find how much your own ease of uniformity of your decisions will depend on a proper attention to judicious forms and regulations. Some other time I shall write more fully on this subject. The house I am building for my own residence is in a great state of forwardness, and very soon hope to become an inhabitant of it ...

Sydney New South Wales 21 September 1811
My Dearest Jeffery,

The Departure of the New Zealander for England (though not direct) affords me an opportunity which I embrace with much pleasure of again writing to you. But it is not my intention to write at length or to any other person by this conveyance. For I understand the New Zealander is again going to the Fishery to fill up, so that the time of her arrival in England is very uncertain. And further, I do not much like these Whalers. The Providence however will leave this Port in three weeks and by her I am writing at great length to all my Friends. I am sending a variety of things home by her, Seeds Birds, etc etc. Though the Providence goes via China, I prefer writing by her because my particular friends Major Cleveland and Captain Piper go home in her, and will be the bearers of my despatches. They have lived in habits of perfect intimacy with us and will be able to inform you minutely of our circumstances, Situation, manner of living etc. I have much pleasure in acknowledging the letters I received by the Cumberland, Providence and Cato, which latter brought one Box for us containing two tin Cases, one of millinery, the other containing a very pretty Dressing case, Books etc etc. They arrived in the best order imaginable. You will I am sure, be all sorry to learn that I had a relapse of my complaint. But let not this depress any of your spirits, for my general health is not affected by it. My appetite is as good as ever. I weigh 14 stone. The principal Inconvenience I feel is that I am very infirm and lame – not able to walk more than half a mile at a time.

But then I can ride 40 miles at a time without fatigue or Inconvenience. Indeed, were you to see me sitting in my chair, or in a Gig, on a horseback, you would swear that nothing was the matter with me. But as poor Pemberton used to say, I do not stand well on my Pins. I am thankful for the Commission I received from the Admiralty, but I think they might have added some Salary to it. What I want very much is the table of Fees in the Prize and Instance Courts of the Admiralty, by the Judges, Registrar, Marshal etc. etc. Continue sending the Admiralty Reports. In two years time I shall be a rich Man; in that time, I shall be desiring an Income a little short of £1000 pr annum from my stock alone, which is remarkably fine, and profitable beyond anything you in England can conceive...To give you some idea of the profit of this kind of stock, a Mr Fitzgerald from the produce of eight Mares from the year 1802 till 1811 cleared £4000 and of Stock in general Mr Mc Arthur sold to the amount of £15,000 in one year without affecting his breeding stock

Wednesday 25 September 1811
The entrance of Major Cleveland and other visitors obliged me to cease writing and the Interval has been employed in an excursion which Eliza and myself made, in company with the Governor and Mrs Macquarie to the town of Liverpool situated upon the Georges River, and to Parramatta. We returned only yesterday and the remainder of that day we passed at Government house. The immediate departure of the Vessel and the letter bag being now kept open purposely for me will compel me to conclude this letter very abruptly. I believe I possess the means of giving to the Publick a most ample account of this colony in every point of view and am about it. But I dare not publish it: for it would certainly contain Observations and Statements which might offend ...

Governor and Mrs Macquarie will sail for the settlement in Van Dieman's land in the course of the next month. I think it a very foolish excursion and am very sorry for it. In my next [letter], I shall dilate upon my situation in every point of view. Of all things in the world, I should like to have an Inside Irish Jaunting car – made neat and strong and light. I could put my two little ones in it so snugly and drive them myself.

Sydney New South Wales 19 October 1811
My Dear Jeffery

This letter will be delivered to you by my most esteemed friend Captain Ovens of the 73rd Regiment accompanied I trust by Captain Piper of the 102nd Regiment. When I say that they are the flowers of our Flock, and were most intimate here, I am sure you be gratified by seeing them. Ovens is the Godfather of my little Boy Robert and in the most handsome manner bought a most beautiful young cow in calf for him on going away, before he gave me the smallest hint of it. He has lived with us almost as a Brother, and a finer, more amiable or more honourable young man, I never knew. I send by him for my mother, an old pet of ours, an excellent white cockatoo, and also some skins of Birds of this country. I have desired Ovens to get pieces of Chinese Crape, one for Ellen and one for Bessy. As the Providence returns via China she will not arrive in England as soon as the Gambier or Friends, by which I write to all largely. God Bless you all, and believe me Dear Jeffery.

I have given them both letters to have and will thank you to introduce them. You must excuse this – but the departure of almost my only and certainly my most valued acquaintances has quite unmanned me. Adieu.

Sydney New South Wales 26 November 1811
My Dearest Mother,

A very long time has now elapsed since I had the pleasure of writing to you ... I will regularly write by India in between which part of the world and New South Wales there is constant communication ... I have had a long and tedious Civil Court, and four Courts of Criminal Judicature and I have none to assist one or with whom to advise. It is too much for me to do well.
... Servants are here more wasteful and do less work by much than in England – you may easily conceive the difficulty of imagining a set of

hardened profligate convicts who are without sense either of shame, or sin, and have long since absconded from every virtuous or moral principle. But, my dear Mother, that you may form a correct estimate of our Expenses, I will give you accurate account and detail of our mode of living. Our family consists of Eliza, myself, Ellis and Robert. I have a Man Cook who does not lodge in the house, and who finds himself in everything, to whom I give £20 pr annum. A Convict Woman of the name of Mary Shorter who came out on the Friends to whom I do not give any fixed wages who is Housemaid another Convict woman who came on the Ship Friends of the name Sarah Smith who is Nursery Maid, and the merest dawdle in natives, a little girl of the Age of 12 or 14 – who is to take care of and play with Ellis in the daytime, and do whatever else she is desired to do. Besides these I have a Convict Man who is my Groom and a free Boy, to wait at table, clean knives and shoes etc. These are the whole of our servants. All our Family[8] including ourselves are victualled from his Majesty's Stores, but you must not therefore suppose that we are supplied with as much meat as we want. A Man's full Ration is eight pounds or four pounds of Pork, 12lbs of wheat and six oz of sugar pr week, A Woman's ¾ of that and a child under a certain Age ½ one under two years ¼. But it sometimes happens that from the scarcity of provisions in the Store, a full ration cannot be issued – and in the above weight of Meat is included a certain quantity of bone. If for instance one gets a Pound of Beef it is always accompanied with an immense shin and so on. I keep in my stable two Horses, one for Eliza, and the other for my Gig, and to carry myself. With the above Assistance I have then to find ten souls with Meat and drink, and nine of them with clothes, washing and lodging. We allow the Servants weekly each 1lb of sugar and 2oz of Tea. Butter of course we do not allow, for we find it a hard matter to get a Pound a week for ourselves. Milk was for some time an expense from 14 to 20 Shillings a week from us. But I have now got a Cow down which supplies at an expence of 1/6 per week. This supply is however but scanty and I mean to have down two cows. I forgot to mention that I have another Government Man whose business it is to find my horses and cows in grass for which purpose I supply him with a Boat. But he has no further claim upon me for anything. Washing here is an article of great expence. The usual price is *four shillings per dozen were I to pay at this Rate It would cost me £130 per year, but instead of that Eliza agrees with a woman to do the whole washing at £60 sterling or £72 colonial money a year.*

By the last returns the Joint Stock of Mr Birch and myself consisted of 672 Head of Sheep and 120 Head of Horned Cattle, my private Stock consists in 24 Head of Horned Cattle two Brood Mares and a filly foal. We have at the farm an excellent deserving old Scotchman who came to this Country, as Overseer, and six men. We have there a comfortable hut, and grow corn sufficiently for our own consumption. We have ten acres of Indian Corn planted this season which will be reaped in April next and will 300 Bushells. The ground being the best in the country – this farm will shortly supply us with Butter, Milk, poultry, eggs and Pork. Our Overseer has £50 per annum and a ration of 6lbs of Pork and 12lbs of Wheat per week, the men have £12 per annum and the same ration. But five out of the six are victualled from the Government Store, so that their ration is merely an additional 2lbs of pork each per week. This year we put into the store 5 Bullocks which brought us £150 sterling, next year we shall put into the store 20 fat Bullocks and shall have for sale 150 sheep. These can all be put into the store at 9d per lb, certain pay by Bills of the Treasury. From this statement I feel justified in concluding that at the expiration of two or three years, I shall be tolerably rich. In less than five years, I shall, if God be willing, be able to rejoin you all and leave a certain and increasing income of £1000 pr annum. Observe Mrs King: she is now living in London and receives remittances from this colony on account of her Horned Cattle of £1500 per annum. It is not more than five years since she began with 100 cows.

I have now, my dear Mother given you a correct detail of our domestick arrangements, and of my situation here and my means of making a provision for my Family.

I am happy in being able to inform you that in concurrence with the Governor's wishes and by his desire I have written a long despatch to Lord Liverpool pointing out to him the imperfections of the Judicial system of this colony, and the necessity of its speedy reform

The Governor in his dispatch has referred his Lordship to my letter, and strongly supported my ideas, and has in the most earnest manner praised my Conduct and recommended that I should have an increased salary of £1500 per annum. What the result will be, I do not know, but the Governor confidently assures me that his private reasons for supposing that this alteration will soon take place. Now let me speak a little of ourselves personally. Eliza I am sorry to say is not so well as I could wish. About the latter end of last month, She had a very severe attack of that most fatal complaint in this country, the Dysentery. She was confined to her bed for some days during which she suffered most excruciating pain. She has got over it but has never been thoroughly well since; she is by no means strong, and has no appetite whatever and expects poor Girl to add one more to my little flock about July next. When she was pregnant with Robert you may recollect she was thrown from her horse and it was but yesterday that the axle of our Gig broke while I was driving her down hill and by the greatest miracle our Lives were spared. Ellis is grown prodigiously and shows strong indications of natural quickness of mind, but I fear he is too lively and volatile to expect much steady application. He now talks very much for a child his Age and is beginning to learn his letters;he will not bear checking except in the mildest manner, and if I show any signs of impatience, or attempt to scold him when he is learning he flies off immediately. He frequently talks of grandpop and grand mama, and says they are over the Water. I sincerely wish he was with you. I am sure you would find him as docile as possible and as tractable. This is a terrible place for children.The departure of the Providence took away three of our most valued friends, Major Cleaveland, Captain Ovens, Captain Piper. Mr Ovens in particular we have much reason to regret…he was quite devoted to the Children and on taking leave of them, cryed, poor fellow! like a child.

I will now endeavour to give you a little chit chat – the Sydney Races took place, on Monday the 12 August. The first prize contended for was 60 guineas given by the Subscribers to the race course. This was won by Match-em (my horse) at two heats beating two other Horses, one of whom was Chace, which won the 50 Guineas and the Cup last year. On the Wednesday Match-em ran for the cup, but somebody or other contrived to get into my Stable before, and gave him green food, which purged him the morning of the Race, and made him quite a different horse. The consequence was, that he was beat and did not run again. The Cup was won by a horse belonging to the Lieut. Governor. I do not mention the other races because you will read an account of them in the papers. But in consequence of some words that took place relative to a subsequent race a Duel took place on Saturday in the Race Course between Mr Campbell, Secretary to the Governor and Captain Richie of the 73rd in which the latter was very severely wounded in the Hip. It was first supposed he was dead, and we were in the utmost confusion, none moreso, than the Governor and myself, but I thank God, His Life has been spared, and he is now out of danger though likely to be lame for Life, as the Ball cannot be extracted. This is not the only Duel that has taken place for a few days ago, a Duel took place between the Commissary and Wm Hadley of the 102 Regt in consequence of a dispute about some water which ended in blood; Lt Hadley being shot through the thigh, the second fire. But besides Duels we have also had a little Crim: Con⁹ Captain Murray soon after the marriage of Lt Col O'Connell, and the death of Lt Governor Collins, was sent down to take the command at the Derwent or Hobart Town, a Settlement of ours in Van Dieman's Land. He took his wife with him, and an only child. Lieut. Wright of the 73rd one of the Officers who went down with him, acted the part of Lothario on this occasion and in consequence a Separation has taken place, and the naughty Lieutenant has been sent up here. I write this lightly on the business because Murray has not altogether acted the part of a good husband, or deserved a virtuous wife: and it was reported that the Lady was not inconstant for the first time and that much higher in the Regiment is the real Lothario. But I know nothing of these matters. 'For what is Hecuba to me or I too Hecuba'. So you see we are very Hyde Parkish. Governor and Mrs Macquarie are gone on what the Governor calls a tour of inspection to our Settlements in Van Dieman's Land, and is not expected to return until the middle of January or beginning of February next. In the meantime this part of the Territory is under the Command of Lt Governor O'Connell. He is now operating under instructions from the Governor which may rather be called restrictions. I am sorry to say My house is not yet finished nor will it be for the nine months. I am sorry I ever engaged in it, not that I shall ever suffer more than anxiety though. The expense will be greater than I expected, I fear the person with whom I contracted will not be able to complete it, indeed I know he will not. But the Governor on account of the increased expense has allowed me to purchase 1000 gallons of spirits at 8s – which I have done and shall sell from 25d per Gallon. I'm sure he will not let me lose by it.

The Ships Indian, Providence, Admiral Gambier, Friends, and Thames, Cumberland and Cato have all arrived since I last wrote and I have now a regular Journal from you from the 23rd May 1809 to the 24 May 1811 which is the last date I received – I cannot describe the gratification, they have afforded me, and if possible, they make me love you ten times more – but I cannot love you more.

PS

I was so fatigued when I concluded my letter last night that I omitted to mention some circumstances which I much wished to mention. In the first place I have sent by Mr Ovens to you a favourite and beautiful Cockatoo Prime – white with a straw coloured crest . He doesn't require any cage, being as domestic as possible but must be crammed,[10] every time he is fed. That however you will choose. I have sent to each of my sisters Bessy and Ellen; or rather I have desired Mr Ovens to purchase in China two pieces of Chinese crape which will make each two dresses. I beg they will accept them as a Poor Man's token of his continued and sincere affection for them. I fear I shall not be able to write them by this opportunity as I have been writing the whole of this day and have still some business letters to get through ... assure them that Eliza joins with me in tenderest love to them. I shall certainly [write] to Charles Knox. I entreat you will give my kind regards to Mr and Mrs D'Oyley, and my warmest thanks for his grateful attention to an old Friend, in sending her pretty urn stands to Eliza, with so kind a note. Tho' there are two, I cannot spare one to anybody. Eliza and I return our kindest thanks to you, for the cheeses, Pickles, Mincemeat and Preserves. Unfortunately the Pickles were all destroyed. The Mincemeat and preserves came very *well – but many things fall out between the cup and the lip. One of my rascally Convict servants (but I have never been able to find out which) before our faces, contrived to avail himself of our anxiety and to steal the Conje pot of preserved Gooseberries. So you see the description of people I have about me. I have sent some Birds, and other things to Mrs Reeve and Mrs Ward.*

My Dearest Mother,

I am now closing my letters, Such a Heap! I have a hard weeks work – and yet feel conscious I have omitted much in my letter to you. I have not answered your letter at all. I have particularly forgotten to mention how much obliged Eliza and myself were to you and Ellen for the Kind trouble you took, about the Commissions all which arrived safe, and in completely good order. We must also thank you for the things which you sent of your own work which were particularly pleasing to Eliza. These instances of Kind attention are most cheering to us, and we had not forgotten them. For I mentioned them in a letter I wrote my Brother, in the New Zealander. Little Robert walks by himself. I have written to Charles, but not my sisters. But another opportunity by way of India will occur in a fortnight of which I will avail myself. We were truly shocked by the account you gave us of Mrs G Knox's death. I wish you had given the particulars … would I could wish you with any probability a merry Xmas, but I will at all events a happy new year – Mrs O'Connell has been about 15 months in a family way for 12 of which she has had her cot, linen. Caps etc etc etc all ready. – but the Mountain will not bring forth even a mouse yet.[11]

P.S I forgot to say I had sent Sydney Gazettes – and a Sydney Almanack – Adieu
This is the last scratch of my pen.

Endnotes

1   Furniture refers to cloth here.
2   Blistering by an ungent was a common practice in eye treatment. H. Corlett, 'No Small Uncertainity, Eye Treatments in Eighteenth Century France and England', *Medical History*, 42, 1998, 217-234.
3   Alexander Berry describes this incident in HRA, 1, 1, vol VII, p. 294.
4   The Embargo Act stopped American ships from engaging in Foreign Trade from 1807-1812. In this case it appears to have prevented importation of goods into New South Wales on an American ship.
5   A centre ornament for a dinner table to hold flowers or fruit.
6   A lunch.
7   This debt to Birch may have been the cause of Bent leaving so little money to his wife.
8   This term included servants.
9   Criminal Connection – meant humorously.
10 Overfed.
11 Humour and gossip re Mary O'Connell's [nee Putland] claim to be pregnant for some months.

SELECT BIBLIOGRAPHY

Atkins, G., *Wilberforce and his Milieux, the Worlds of Anglican Evangelicalism c1780-1830*, PDF Cambridge, online, 2007.

Atkinson, A., *The Europeans in Australia, A History, Volume One,* Oxford University Press, Melbourne, 1998.

Atkinson, Alan, 'Richard Atkins The Women's Judge', *Journal of Australian Colonial History*, Vol 1, No 1 pp. 115-142.

Austen, J., *Pride and Prejudice,* Penguin, Harmondsworth, 1972.

Austen, J., *Sense and Sensibility,* Penguin, Harmondsworth, 1969.

Australian Dictionary of Biography, National Centre of Biography, ANU, Canberra.

Boswell, James, *The Journal of a Tour to the Hebrides with Samuel Johnson,* Macdonald, London, 1785.

Byrne, P., 'The Public Good: Competing Visions of Freedom in Colonial New South Wales', *Labour History*, May 1990, pp. 76-83.

Castles, A.C., *An Australian Legal History*, Law Book Co., Sydney, 1982.

Chatterton, K., *Sailing Ships*, Sidgewick and Jackson, London, 1914.

Currey, C.H., *The Brothers Bent*, Sydney University Press, Sydney, 1968.

Dening, G., *Mr Bligh's Bad Language,* Cambridge University Press, New York, 1992.

Dictionary of National Biography, Vol XX, Macmillan, London, 1885.

Goodwin, P., *Men O' War,* Carlton Books, 2003.

Heal, F., *Hospitality in Early Modern England,* Clarendon, Oxford, 1990, pp. 6-15.

Historical Records of Australia (HRA), Series I and IV

Ikegami, E., *Bonds of Civility, Aesthetic Networks and the Political Origins of Japanese Culture,* Cambridge University Press, Cambridge, 2005.

Katz, J.E. and Aakhus, M., *Perpetual Contact,* Cambridge University Press, Cambridge, 2002.

Kercher, B., *An Unruly Child, A History of Law in Australia*, Allen and Unwin, Sydney, 1995.

Mackaness, G., *Sir Joseph Banks*, Sydney University Press, Sydney, 1936.

Martin, J., *An Account of the Natives of the Tonga Islands of the South Pacific,* Charles Ewer, Boston, 1820.

McIntyre, J., 'Bannelong sat down with Governor Phillip and drank his wine and coffee as usual, Aborigines and wine', *History Australia*, Vol. 5, No. 2, 2008, 39 e-text.

McMartin, A., *Public Servants and Patronage*, Sydney University Press, Sydney, 1983.

Moreton Robinson, A., 'I still call Australia Home: Indigenous belonging and place in a white postcolonizing society' in S. Ahmed, C. Cantaneda, A.M. Furtier and M. Sheller eds., *Uprootings/Regroundings, Questions of Home and Migration*, Berg, Oxford, 2003.

Naish, G.P.B and Amery, H., *The Age of Sailing Ships*, Usborne, Chicago, 1976.

O'Neill, R., *Patrick O'Brien's Navy*, Salamander Books, Baltimore, 2003.

Pratt, M., *Imperial Eyes*, Routledge, London,1992.

Ritchie, J., *Lachlan Macquarie, A Biography*, Melbourne University Press, Melbourne, 1986.

Rosen, L., *Law As Culture*, Princeton University Press, Princeton, 2006.

The Times, London.

Selwyn, D., *Jane Austen and Leisure*, Hambledon Press, London, 1999.

Shaw, A.G.L., *Convicts and the Colonies,* Faber, London, 1966.

Styles, J., *The Dress of the People,* Yale University Press, London, 2007.

Thorne, R.G., *The House of Commons, 1790–1820*, History of Parliament Trust, Secker and Warburg, London, 1986

Tindale Daniell, T., *The Lawyers*, Gray's Inn, London, 1971.

INDEX